THE ART OF THE
NEEDLE

THE ART OF THE NEEDLE

DESIGNING IN FABRIC AND THREAD

JAN BEANEY

CENTURY

LONDON SYDNEY AUCKLAND JOHANNESBURG

Dedicated to past and present embroidery students
of Windsor and Maidenhead College of Further Education

Edited by Eleanor Van Zandt
Designed by Sue Storey
Photography by Dudley Moss
Fashion Photography by Tony Boase
Fashion Styling by Jackie Boase
Make-up and Hair by Rod at Select Model Agency
Modelling by Diane Howard
Still Life Photography on pages 44, 47, 49 and 85 by Andreas von Einsiedel
Styling for photography on pages 44, 47, 49 and 85 by Totty Whately
Stitch Illustrations by Dennis Hawkins

First published in 1988 by Century Hutchinson Ltd,
Brookmount House, 62–65 Chandos Place, Covent Garden,
London WC2N 4NW

Century Hutchinson Australia Pty Ltd,
89–91 Albion Street, Surry Hills, Sydney,
NSW 2010, Australia

Century Hutchinson New Zealand Ltd,
PO Box 40–086, Glenfield, Auckland 10,
New Zealand

Century Hutchinson South Africa Pty Ltd,
PO Box 337, Bergvlei,
2012 South Africa

British Library Cataloguing in Publication Data

Beaney, Jan
   The art of the needle: designing in
   fabric and thread
   1. Embroidery – Manuals
   I. Title
   746.44

   ISBN 0 7126 1942 9

Printed and bound in Italy by
New Interlitho Spa Milan

Detail of a panel by Karen Fleming. Applied sheer fabrics and machine
embroidery on vanishing muslin and water soluble fabric.

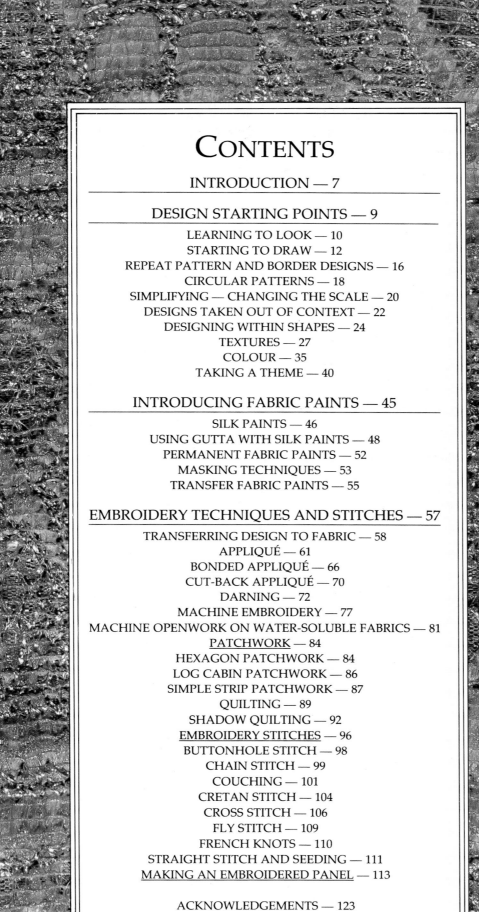

CONTENTS

INTRODUCTION

At exhibitions and classes on embroidery I am constantly reminded how excited people become when looking at and touching fabrics and threads. The fabulous colours and textures available and the wide variety of techniques in which they can be incorporated never fail to intrigue people.

Once you become fascinated with the materials, you will experience an overwhelming desire to work in this medium. To enable you to make that first step towards making your own fabric and thread creations, the first part of this book shows you how to look for inspiration in the patterns, textures and colour schemes around you, and how to translate this inspiration into designs. The following sections show you how to colour and pattern fabrics and explain some methods of transferring your designs onto the fabric. The remaining sections describe a selection of embroidery techniques, thus giving you the opportunity to experiment and to build up and broaden your knowledge and so create your own exciting embroidered images. The techniques are explained in sufficient detail to enable you to complete a project using that medium, or perhaps combining two or three different media.

Embroidery is a wonderfully varied art form, and no single book can hope to describe all of its many techniques in depth. (The specialist books listed on page 126 will help you to explore certain techniques further.) The aim of this book is, rather, to inspire you to try those techniques that are new to you, and, if you are already adept at working in some media, to try being a bit more adventurous in your use of them. For example, if you were taught to work embroidery stitches precisely, see what interesting effects you can achieve by working them freely.

But above all, it is my hope that this book may help you to become more aware of – and to enjoy – the colours and textures that surround you in your daily life.

This appliqué panel, using a variety of green fabrics, was inspired by a decorative surround of a doorway and worked in straight machine stitches.

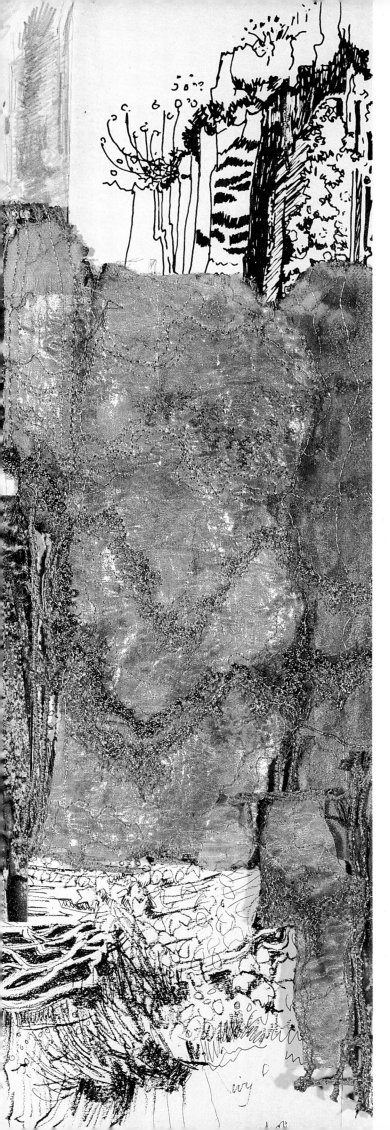

DESIGN STARTING POINTS

Many people are reluctant to design their own embroidery because they lack confidence in their creative ability. In particular, they are frightened of drawing.

The aim of this first section is to dispel such fears. First of all, there are many different approaches to designing, and among them you are sure to find at least one that suits you. Tracings of photographs, collage and cut paper shapes can all be employed in the development of a design idea. Secondly, it is not necessary to create beautiful, finished drawings; for embroidery purposes, all you need to be able to do is to observe your surroundings keenly and to record helpful information. In this section you will learn how to make small sketches focusing on details of a subject which will be of enormous use in planning a piece of embroidery. Keep these jottings and sketches in a sketchbook for future reference, along with photographs, diagrams and written descriptions. Scraps of fabric and technique experiments can also go into your stockpile of design ideas.

In addition to a sketchbook you will need just a few drawing materials. A medium-soft pencil or a fibre-tip pen will serve for noting line and texture; but the addition of colour will make your sketches more exciting and useful. The best paint for your purpose is gouache, an opaque, water-based paint (also called 'designer's colour'). The three primary colours – red, blue and yellow – plus black and white – will do at the outset.

You might also try some of the wonderful water-soluble coloured pencils now available. Allow yourself time to learn, and with practice you will gain the skills and confidence to create your own unique designs in fabric and thread.

These studies of a rock face – photographs; sketches in a variety of media including paint, pencil and crayon; and experiments in fabric bonding (see page 66) – reveal some of the careful observation that goes into designing an embroidery.

LEARNING TO LOOK

The most important starting point in design is to learn to look. We all think that we are observant until we are asked to make a sketch or diagram of a particular object. Do you really know how branches grow out from a tree trunk, or how many colours and patterns are contained within your garden fence? What shapes and textures are exposed when you slice open fruits and vegetables, or can be viewed through your windowpanes? Your front door, a chimney pot, a kitchen gadget, or the markings on a leaf can all be observed and recorded by means of a simple sketch diagram. These, in turn, can be developed into interesting motifs to be arranged and repeated in a number of attractive patterns, many of which can be interpreted in a wide range of embroidery techniques.

Jot down ideas, shapes and descriptions on the back of an envelope or in a notebook; or better still, start keeping a sketchbook. Use a camera to get some back-up reference if you are short of time, or describe in words the scene or object you are looking at. Become an avid observer, and set yourself specific exercises to sharpen your visual powers. For instance, note the range of greens to be seen in your garden: the grass and foliage may contain colours ranging from khaki and lime to blue-greens, grey-greens and emerald. Observe the variety of leaf shapes in your collection of house plants, or the pleasing patterns contained within stone or wood carvings in churches, old houses or museums. Look at the range of roof tiles, drainpipes and building materials to be seen in your neighbourhood. Be aware of the effects of the weather. For example, rain intensifies the colour differences on tree bark or slate roofs, whereas snow and ice can transform a garden into a shimmering, silvery-white scene.

These looking exercises, including your sketches and written descriptions, will greatly increase your powers of observation, and will help you to overcome any hesitation about starting to make your own designs.

Enjoy looking around and about yourself. You will be amazed at the richness of colour and pattern that surrounds you in everyday life.

The richness of colour and pattern found in nature is suggested (opposite) by a cut section of a pepper, lacy leaves and delicate blossoms, set against the pattern of veins in a leaf.

Both natural and man-made objects provide endless sources of inspiration for the embroiderer. This splendid statue of an eagle (above) at Cliveden House, Berkshire, with its bold, distinctive shape, is well suited to a stylized cut-paper border pattern (right).

STARTING TO DRAW

These sketches of a flower (below) show how an ellipse shape can be used to put the blossom into perspective and indicate the foreshortening of the petals, and how a simple diagrammatic sketch can be used to represent the proportions of stem and blossom and their relationship to each other.

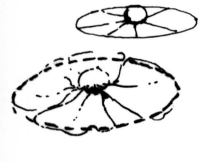

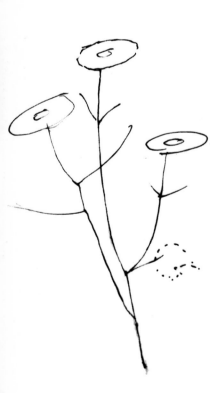

After learning to really look at things around you in everyday life, developing a visual curiosity and jotting down your observations, the next stage is, inevitably, starting to draw.

It is a commonly held myth that the ability to draw well is something one is born with and does naturally. Most people accept that mastery of mathematics, foreign languages or a musical instrument necessitates practising carefully structured exercises which build up the student's confidence and skill and lead on to advanced knowledge. So it is with drawing and painting; exercises in these skills can also be devised and structured in the same way. You can learn to draw to a competent standard – and certainly well enough to record the aspects of a particular object or view that most appeal to you. The following section will, it is hoped, start you off in the right direction.

Before you undertake the task of drawing, for example, a house, a still life or a landscape, first do some preparatory research. Without having experience, attempting such ambitious projects could put you off drawing forever. Train yourself to ask questions, such as those listed below, about the object or view you are observing. Allow time to get to know the subject you are about to draw. Having devised a list of questions, systematically work through them by sketching areas and details out of context. Not only will you then gain experience of really looking and drawing what you can see – rather than what you think you can see – but your actual drawing skills will improve, as well as your ability to relate one shape to another within their context. Try using varying drawing media, such as soft and medium water-soluble pencils, pen and wash (thin watercolour or ink), different coloured crayons and paper shapes, cut

freehand and stuck down; all have particular qualities to offer.

The following lists related to observing plants and buildings have been included to suggest how you can devise questions to help you observe any type of subject.

GETTING TO KNOW A PLANT

1. Draw the outline of a single petal.
2. Count the number of petals. Jot down notes about the quality of a petal. Has it a waxy, satiny, papery or velvety texture?
3. How do the petals overlap and join the centre of the flower?
4. How does the flower join the stem?
5. How do the leaves join the stem?

6. Draw the outline of a single leaf. Take particular note of the edge. Is it crinkly, indented, crisp or hairy? Has it been partially eaten away?
7. Sketch several leaves, taking note of the background spaces; these will help you to relate one leaf to another.
8. Draw the centre of the flower out of context.
9. Note the spaces, if any, between the petals.
10. Draw the whole flower, looking carefully at the proportions of the petals to the centre.
11. Try observing the flower from varying viewpoints, and sketch in guideline ellipses to help indicate the foreshortening of the petals.
12. Make a simple diagrammatic sketch of the whole flower or plant, using lines for

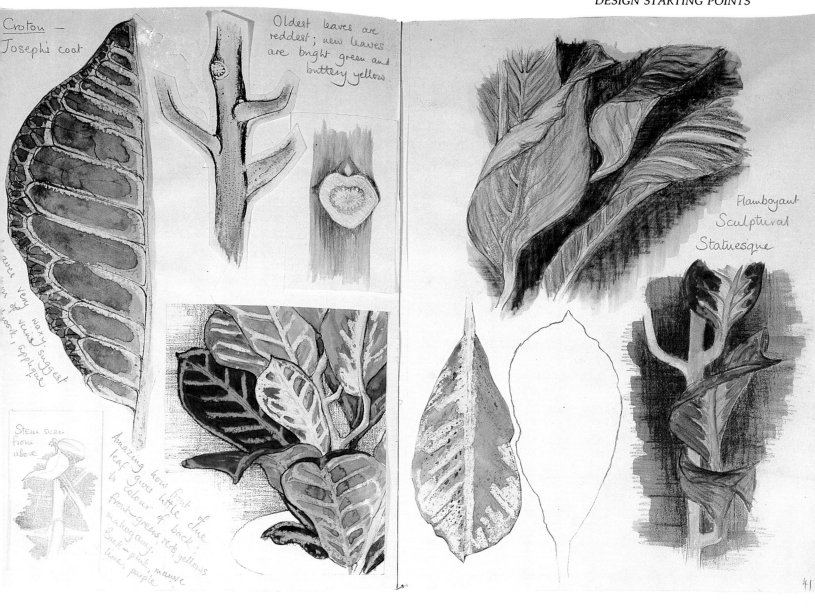

Croton —
Joseph's coat

Oldest leaves are
reddest; new leaves
are bright green and
buttery yellow

leaves very waxy, suggest
... of veins ... look, appliqué

Stem seen
from
above

Amazing how front of
leaf gives little clue
to colour of back;
front—greens, reds, yellows
mahogany;
back—pink, mauve
lime, purple

Flamboyant
Sculptural
Statuesque

41

stems and circles or ovals for petals and
leaves, and taking care to observe the relative
sizes of these elements.

13. Using a magnifying glass if necessary,
draw patterns out of context. The stamens,
the vein pattern within a leaf, the texture of a
stalk and markings in the petals could all
serve as intriguing sources of design.

14. If you like, follow up this examination by
making paint prints from the petals or leaves
or cutting simple paper patterns featuring
certain aspects of the plant.

15. Attempt a drawing of the whole flower
or plant, remembering to sketch in the main
proportions and shapes first. Check background spaces between the flowers, leaves
and stems before adding the details.

16. Finally, add notes on colour and texture,
as well as suggestions for fabrics or stitches
suitable for interpreting your observations.

*The rich colours and
striking patterns of this
luxuriant croton plant
(opposite) might present
a somewhat daunting
challenge to a beginner
attempting to draw it. But
by studying individual
parts of the plant, as has
been done in this sketchbook
(above), it is possible to
build up a thorough visual
understanding of the plant
as a whole. Water-soluble
coloured pencils have been
used to convey the intense
colours, and a few verbal
notes ('statuesque',
'sculptural', 'buttery
yellow', etc.) reinforce the
visual studies.*

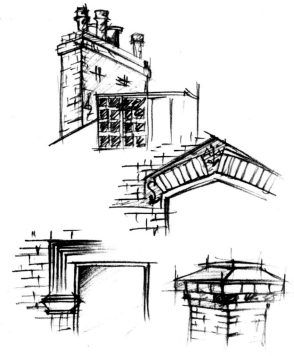

GETTING TO KNOW A BUILDING

Stand back and view the building. Then, starting at the top, answer each question with a diagram, sketch or relevant notes. There is no need to draw every brick, ridge tile, stone or small windowpane. Jot down enough information to help you at a future date.

1. What sort of line does the top of the building make against the sky? Are there any chimneys, turrets or spires? Make a simple line diagram showing the building silhouetted against the sky. Look carefully at the 'sky' shapes, as these observations can help you to relate the parts of the building.

2. Make a simple outline drawing of a chimney or spire out of context.

3. What sort of roof is it? It could be flat, gabled, castellated or pitched at an acute angle.

4. Look at the material used for the roof. Is it glass, corrugated iron, thatch or slate? Draw the types of ridge or roof tile if they feature. Remember to add notes on colour and texture. An old rusty corrugated tin roof could be eroding into holes or covered in clumps of moss, whereas a wet slate roof could be shining and subtly coloured in a range of blue, grey, purple, silver and pink.

5. Notice the drainpipes, gutters and general pipework. On some medieval buildings ornate gargoyles decorate the drainpipes.

6. What is the main part of the building made of? Is it brick, flintstone or glass; or is it clad in patterned tiles, cement blocks, timbers or shingles?

7. Make a close-up sketch of one brick, a flintstone or a tile pattern to familiarize yourself with the amazing range of colour that can be found in one tiny component.

8. Draw one window. Take note of its overall shape before adding details of windowpanes, pediments or brick surrounds.

9. Sketch the main doorway, following the same procedure. In this case there could be more decorative features to highlight. Panelling, windowpanes set in and around

The sketches on these pages illustrate the process of studying the features of a building before attempting to draw the building as a whole. Note the use of guide lines to establish the slant of a roof or the perspective of a chimney before actually drawing the feature. Written descriptions of the colours have been added to assist the memory when interpreting the sketch.

the door, a doorknob, a knocker, a letterbox, a house number, a lamp, a pot plant, a porch with carved balustrading could all be aspects worth sketching out of context.

10. When you feel that you know the general characteristics of the building, then you can stand back and attempt to draw the whole structure.

11. Lightly draw or block in the main lines of the building. Is it a tall, thin building, or is it low and long? Follow this by suggesting the main proportions of the biggest shapes, such as the roof, windows and doors. Check your lines by looking at the spaces of the walls between the windows and door.

12. When you are satisfied with the overall appearance, then proceed to add the other features and their details.

13. Add notes on colour and texture and ideas for fabric, thread and stitches.

As you can see from the illustrations included throughout the book, details and sections taken out of context can be the start of some attractive pieces of work, both functional and decorative. Once you have started making your own designs, the commercial kits available may lose some of their appeal.

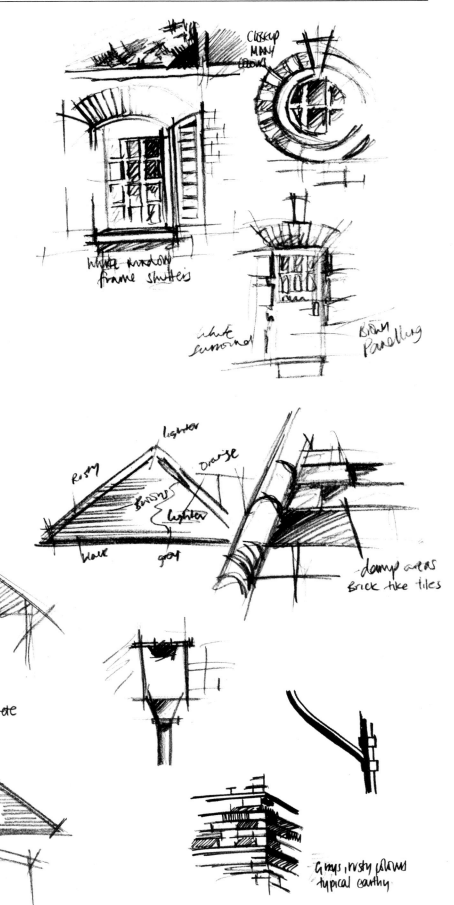

REPEAT PATTERN AND BORDER DESIGNS

All sorts of ordinary objects found around the house can be adapted to form repeat patterns, as the designs on this page – based on a chair, an individual mince pie and a kitchen scale – demonstrate.

Motifs suitable for border designs and repeat patterns can be devised using one of several simple methods. First collect together some sketches, photographs or magazine cuttings, and from these select an image that appeals to you. Begin by drawing the overall shape on a piece of paper, indicating the outside edges and main proportions. When you are satisfied with the general look, add the details. Next, carefully cut out the shape. Use this as a template to cut out several identical shapes from several thicknesses of paper. Alternatively, you can use a photocopying machine to print off the motifs very quickly. Once you have a number of paper shapes, arrange them in a variety of patterns until you achieve a pattern you like.

Some people prefer to bypass the drawing stage and cut the desired shape directly from the paper, even if it takes several attempts to achieve the required effect. This method encourages one to aim for a simple shape, free of unnecessary details.

Another method is to cut a long strip of paper and fold it concertina- or accordion-style. Draw a simple design on the front section only, ensuring that at least one part of the design links on each fold of the paper. Cut out the motif through all the layers of paper. When extended, this should result in a linked, repeating border pattern which may be suitable for a variety of projects.

POINTS TO REMEMBER

● If the motif is too solid, a smaller detail may need to be cut away to break up the large blank area. For example, the kitchen scales illustrated would have been less interesting if the circle representing the dial had not been indicated.

● Objects or motifs with unusual or uneven edges often make good repeating patterns.

● Limit the background spaces and link the shapes together. By doing so, you will often cause unexpected but pleasing patterns to emerge from the background shapes. This action also helps to link the motifs into a unified design.

● Patterns with the same-sized shapes and spaces can be boring. Contrast large and small areas.

● Sometimes the background spaces will appeal to you more than the original motif; these can be emphasized to form a pleasing design.

● If you wish to make the motifs symmetrical, there is an easy way of achieving a good result. Fold a piece of paper in half. Draw one half of the desired motif along the fold; then, keeping the paper folded, cut along the drawn line. When you open out the paper you will have an exactly symmetrical motif.

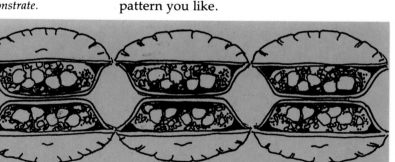

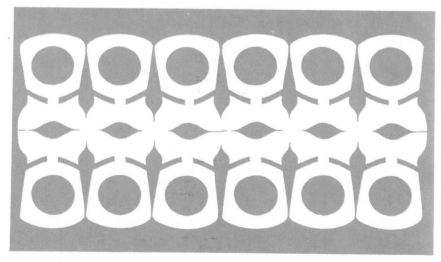

Flowers and plants are, of course, an inexhaustible source of motifs. Tulips provided the shapes for the border design (above), which was stencilled onto fabric, left. The bluebell design below was adapted to decorate the tablecloths on pages 19 and 94.

CIRCULAR PATTERNS

Circular designs can be constructed even from such unlikely objects as a ring pull from a soft drink can (below) and a desk lamp (below, right). A tulip and the leaf markings on a houseplant inspired the other designs (right).

A cut-paper design based on a sketch of bluebells was used for the shadow-quilted tablecloth (opposite). The motifs were cut from fine cotton and sandwiched between two layers of polyester voile. A different treatment of this motif can be seen on page 94.

To create circular patterns, repeat the same initial procedure as for the border designs shown on the previous pages. Experiment with several patterns, as some motifs are more suited than others to circular arrangements. Remember to consider the background spaces as integral parts of the design.

Effective circular designs can also be created by cutting out a circle of paper, perhaps using a plate or saucer as a template to ensure accuracy. Fold the circle into eight sections. With the paper still folded, draw an outline shape on the top segment, making sure that the design extends to the edges at one or more points to prevent it from disintegrating when opened out. Cut along the lines of the drawing, then open the circle to reveal the complete design.

Circular motifs can be combined in all sorts of ways; overlapping them and enlarging or reducing them in relation to each other are some of the possibilities.

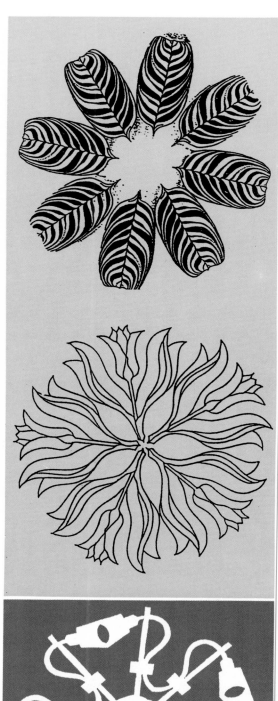

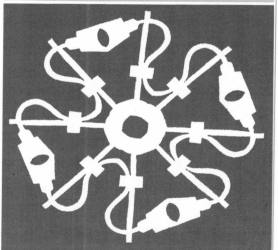

SIMPLIFYING – CHANGING THE SCALE

These colourful repeating patterns (below) *were adapted from the decorations on an Egyptian mummy case. The sketches were enlarged and reduced as required, using a photocopier, and arranged to make an allover pattern. Clear gutta (see page 48) was used to define the design lines on the fabric, and then silk paints were flooded into the shapes.*

When using an object as a source for an embroidery design, remember that you can take all sorts of liberties with it; don't feel that you must be too literal. Simplifying the object will often produce an image that is more suitable for a design. You can also produce interesting variations on a motif by altering its scale. By mixing large and smaller versions of a motif or border pattern within the same design, you can often create a simple, unified and effective arrangement.

Once you take this free, creative approach to design material, you may be surprised to discover how useful, from a design standpoint, quite ordinary objects can be. For example, your kitchen can offer a vast range of design ideas. Cooking utensils, gadgets of all types and, especially, food can be simplified to produce intriguingly shaped patterns. When used as a repeating unit, such a pattern can be the starting point for projects worked in a variety of techniques, such as appliqué and quilting.

Slices of fruit and vegetable often reveal interesting patterns. Having found one that you like, make a simple diagram. First draw the outline of the shape, and then indicate the other major patterns. Pips or larger seeds and other details can be drawn in last. Remember that this exercise is simply to record basic information.

The shape of the lemon slices on the next page was achieved by drawing around a small cup. The segments and pips were drawn freehand, as they are rarely uniform in shape. After drawing one design that you like, copy it by tracing or by photocopying to give yourself a number of identical pieces which you can arrange in different patterns. Limit the size of the background shapes

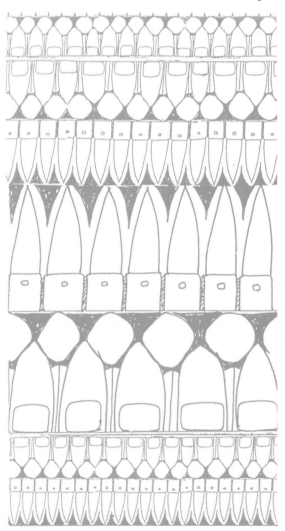
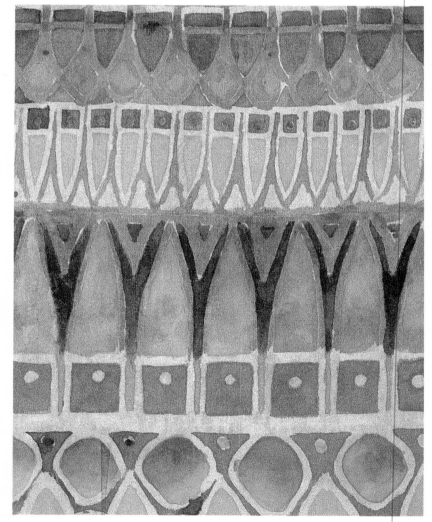

(see page 24) so that your design has unity.

Sometimes a simple design may appear a little boring. If yours does, check that you have observed the original object carefully and have included a few small details to contrast with the larger shapes. An extra line, a change of texture or emphasizing one section of the pattern could improve the design.

Another useful exercise is to vary the scale of the motif. The lemon cushion shows this approach. The small fruits in the outer row contrast with the bolder sections in the central square. Extra lines have been added to link the shapes. This method of designing can result in a wide range of exciting patterns.

A cross-section of a lemon, suitably enlarged and reduced, provided the motif for the hand-quilted silk cushion (below). The quilting was worked by hand, using backstitch and silk buttonhole twist.

DESIGNS TAKEN OUT OF CONTEXT

A wooden trellis served as a frame for viewing the bare branches of a bush in winter (below)*. The pattern enclosed within one square was then sketched and repeated in columns to form the design.*

A comparatively easy and appealing method of designing is to take inspiration from a section of pattern taken out of context by means of a paper or cardboard frame. Your chosen segment of pattern may be acceptable as a 'one-off' composition, a possible design for a picture. Or, if assembled as repeating units, it could be suitable for a cushion or quilt. This approach to design can result in unusual and often quite unexpected creations.

Make a selection of frames by cutting squares and rectangles of varying sizes from scraps of paper or thin cardboard; initially make the openings in the 5–8cm (2–3inch) range. Using one of your sketches, a photograph or a magazine picture as a source for the design, move one of the frames over it to isolate one or more interesting features. Look for contrasting, different-sized shapes. The patterns should also have a focal point, which may be a highlight of unexpected colour or texture. Try another frame if the first yields nothing suitable.

Having chosen a possible source of design, trace the main shapes of that section to see if they still please you when seen in isolation. Repeat the process to find other patterns, if possible, in the picture.

If a repeat pattern is required, trace the image several times, or use the first tracing as a pattern to cut several, until you find the arrangement that appeals to you most. You

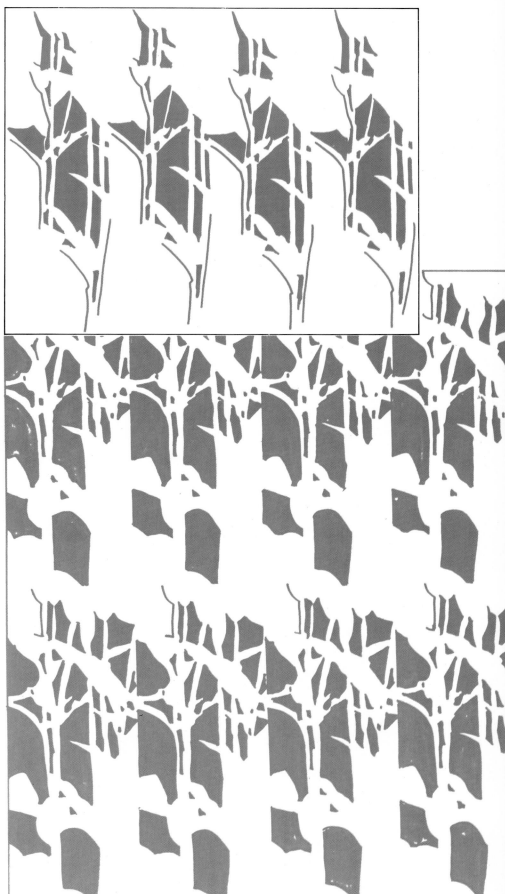

will find that surprising shapes emerge as the sections are linked together. Enlarge the design, if necessary, using the squaring-up method (see page 59) or a photocopier.

An alternative method of taking a design out of context is to use the background, or negative, shapes. Following the same procedure described above, select an interesting arrangement of forms, but in this case highlight the background spaces by shading these in as shown. In many cases these patterns, when repeated, could be interpreted most successfully in appliqué or quilting.

Paper frames were used to select two interesting groups of shapes from this snapshot of a flower border (above). The background spaces between the leaves and the stems made up the pattern, which was then repeated to form an allover pattern. Note that in this case it is the negative spaces – the background – that are featured, whereas the branch design (opposite) emphasizes the positive shapes.

DESIGNING WITHIN SHAPES

These stylized paper cuts of a butterfly (below) illustrate one way of adapting a motif to fit a given shape. Paper cutting is a good method to use for a flat, linear motif such as this.

It is important to consider how a design fits within a given shape. The proportions and positioning of a design that would naturally fit one shape would have to be adjusted and possibly rearranged to fit another. For instance, a circular design would need to be altered to fit a triangular or rectangular shape, or a collar.

Designs cut from paper, like those shown here, can often be ideal in this respect, for the very character of paper cutting dictates a degree of simplicity, which lessens the chance of allowing the pattern to become too complex and encourages you to concentrate on the shape as a whole.

First cut a piece of paper the size and shape you require. Draw the motif on it, extending or exaggerating certain aspects to fit the shape. Concentrate on the shapes to be cut out – that is, the negative spaces – not on those that will remain; this will help to prevent the design from being too complicated. But take care not to leave large, uninteresting background spaces.

If you are planning a symmetrical motif, fold the shaped paper down the centre. Open the paper flat and draw one half of your motif on one side, again accentuating certain elements to fit the shape. Re-fold the paper and, following the design lines on the one side, cut out the shape through both layers. Remember to place the middle of the design on the fold. Then open out the paper, and you will have created a symmetrical image.

Asymmetrical designs can be achieved by selecting sections out of context, using a paper frame of the required shape (see page 22). If you do not feel happy drawing freehand, try distorting your pattern into the desired shape by using the grid system. Following the same method used to enlarge a design (see page 66), draw a grid of equal divisions across your design. Decide on the new shape – whether it should be long and narrow, broad or circular – and draw the outer shape, full

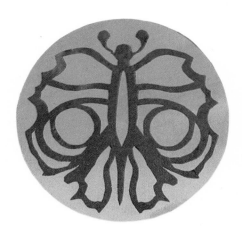

size. Divide this area into sections, the same number as those in the grid over the original drawing. This will produce a grid with rectangular spaces instead of the squares on the original. Transpose the lines of the design onto the new grid, working systematically across it, one section at a time, adjusting the angles of the lines as dictated by the new grid, and taking care to link them up.

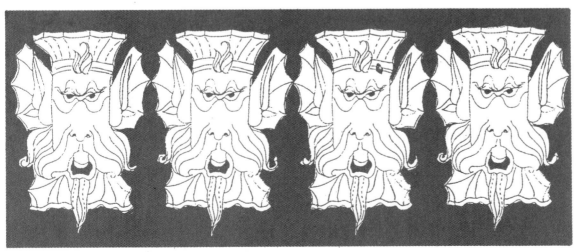

The grotesque stone face (top) on a fountain at Cliveden House was the starting point for some even more grotesque faces, achieved by means of a distorted version of the grid enlargement method described on page 59. This technique of adjusting a motif to fit a shape can yield fascinating results.

TEXTURES

Train yourself to observe the assorted surfaces that surround you in your everyday environment. The wealth of textures to be found will amaze you.

This photograph of sunflower seedheads offers a marvellous range of interesting surfaces. The delicate honeycomb structure, the smooth, elegantly marked seeds, the crunchy area of withered stamens, the papery quality of the sepals and the brittleness of the dying leaf contrast well with the metallic paper against which the arrangement is placed. The basic shapes might first be interpreted in fabric paints, then perhaps enhanced by applying carefully chosen fabrics. The rough textures could be suggested with crunchy areas of stitchery.

These dried sunflower heads (opposite) contain a wealth of texture that could inspire a piece of embroidery. Rusty fences, too, often show a wonderful range of colours and textures. The example below was the starting point for the embroidery bottom, which was created by colouring felt with fabric paint and then working over it with machine and hand embroidery, using a variety of glossy and metallic threads.

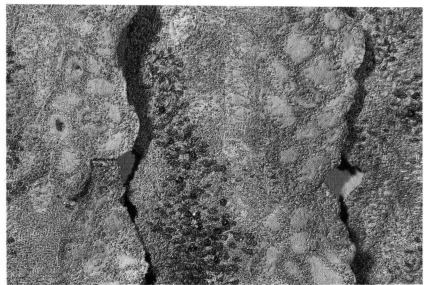

Look at the many types of tree trunk in your neighbourhood, and jot down your observations. Describe in words whether the surface is smooth, banded like ribbons, peeling, patchy, twisted, ridged or distorted into oddly shaped lumps and protrusions. Having noticed the general structure, add further notes and diagrams. Is the bark hairy, or pitted, or does it suggest a string-like quality? List the colours, their proportions and any other features, such as lichen or fungi, that you may wish to emphasize. The notes you keep could help you in making your initial decisions at the outset of an embroidery project.

The fascinating variety of textures and patterns found in tree bark and roots (opposite) can be interpreted in many different ways. One of the most effective is free darning. In the example shown right, above, *softly coloured threads and cords have been freely darned into a coarsely woven scrim. The loose weave of the cloth has allowed the thicker yarns to push the ground threads close together in some areas to produce the flowing lines. In the example at* right, below, *the darning, worked in shaded wool and cotton threads, has been built up in layers to suggest the deep furrows of the bark.*

Twisted tree trunks, like the ones in these sketches, also have linear and textural interest with potential for embroidery.

Follow your first observations by indicating with simple line sketches the most obvious pattern of movement within the bark. This might consist of long, flowing or entwining thick and thin lines suggestive of a plant's root system, or more tightly curved patterns, like the contour lines on a topographic map. The tree trunks you are looking at may contain deep fissures or be covered with wart-like nodules. Note the shape and intensity of the darker-toned areas. Correctly observed and recorded, these will help to reveal the sculptured or raised sections and so emphasize the knotty, gnarled surface.

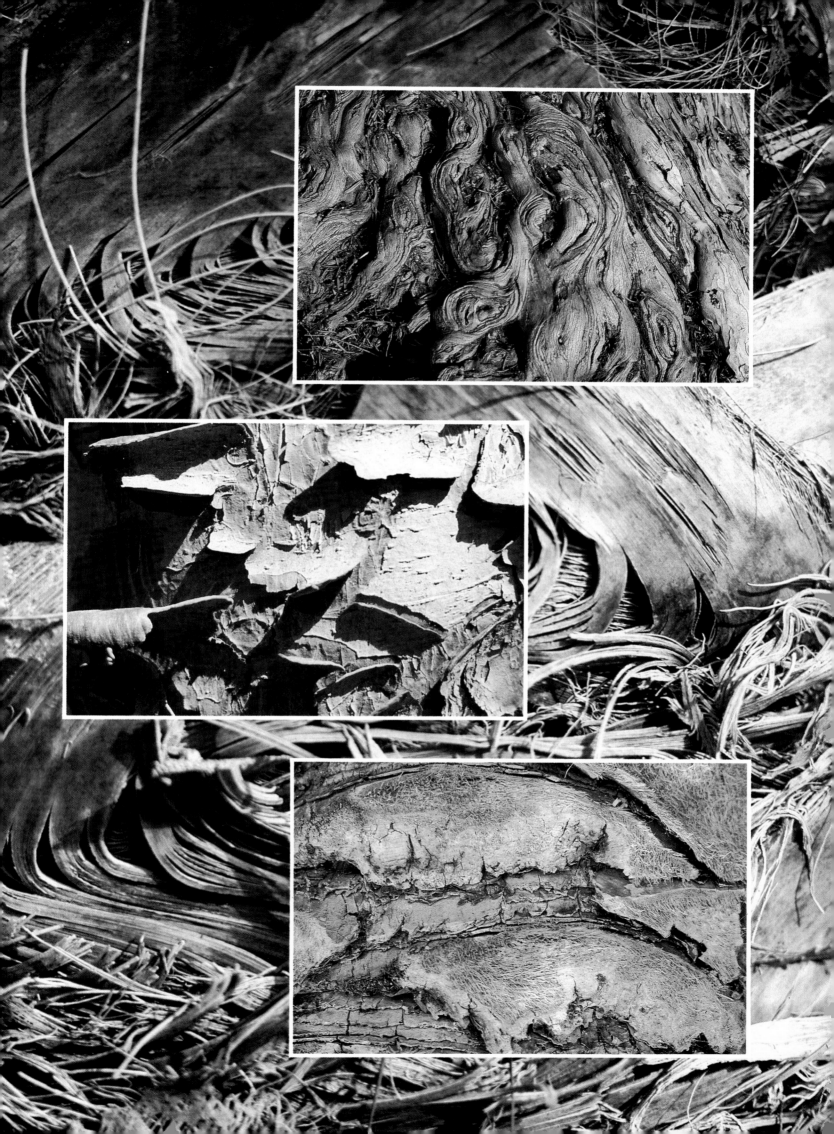

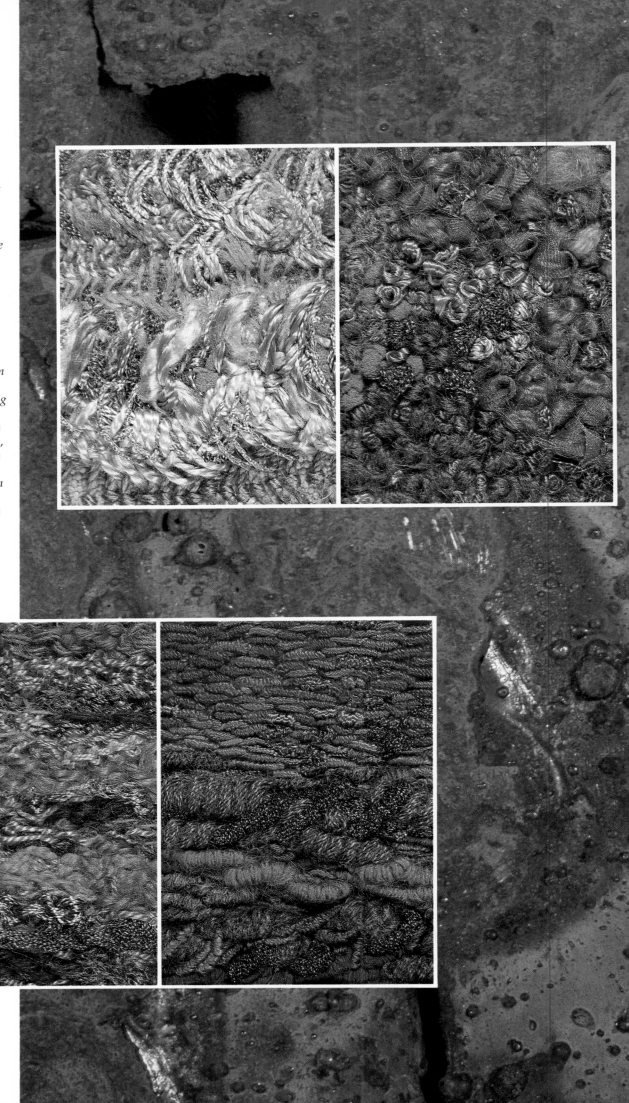

Even such unpromising material as an old corrugated iron fence can contain interesting textures: surfaces weathered by the seasons or eaten away by the effect of corrosive materials to reveal a lacy network of irregular holes. Decorative patterns can be created by shadows cast from curls of peeling multicoloured paints, contrasting with the glistening gossamer gold tracery of the rust, just visible beneath the subdued colours. The samples of stitchery shown here, worked in a variety of embroidery and knitting yarns, demonstrate some of the ways these textures can be interpreted. Right, clockwise from top left: *fly stitch, French knots, bullion knots, raised chain band.* Opposite, clockwise from top left: *couching, buttonhole stitch cross stitch, chain and detached chain.*

30

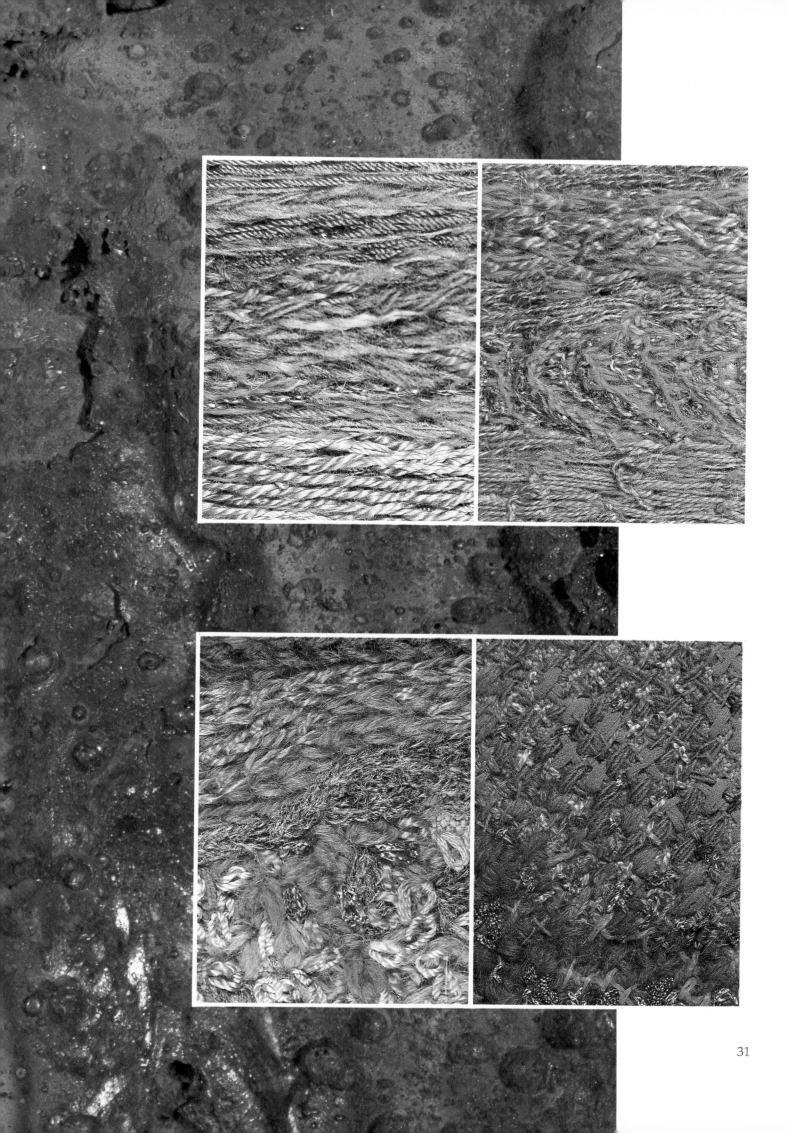

A snapshot of leaves and grasses (above) could be the basis for an interesting study of textures.

'Meadow Grasses', by Julia Caprara, illustrates the use of long, sweeping straight stitches, in a variety of subtly coloured threads, to build up layers of texture and an impression of movement, over a background of fabric-painted calico (unbleached muslin). Round detached chain stitches and loosely worked French knots have been added to suggest wind-borne seeds.

Your careful observations of a view, photograph or sketch will not only reveal its textural qualities but also suggest suitable fabrics, threads and techniques for its interpretation. For example, 'lush', 'shiny', 'smooth', 'glistening' and 'matt' could be some of the words you might use to describe the landscape shown above; and these words, in turn, could assist you in making an appropriate choice of materials. You need not restrict yourself to materials sold in needlework departments. Explore the possibilities of dressmaking and furnishing fabrics – thick, hairy tweeds; slubbed dupions; corded and ridged weaves; smooth cotton and silk; shiny and shot (iridescent) satins and taffetas; and gossamer sheers. Yarns and threads, too, come in a mouth-watering range of textures, from glossy stranded cottons and silks to thick, slubbed knitting yarns. Begin making a collection of these materials for interpreting design ideas.

Examine your chosen subject further to see what its textures suggest in terms of technique. The movement of leaves and grasses in the landscape above might call to mind the words 'crosshatching', 'encroaching' and 'layers', and so suggest freely worked stitches, built up in layers to form a dense texture of threads. A different subject might call for the soft, tactile qualities of quilting. As you expand your range of techniques you will discover many possibilities for interpreting textures.

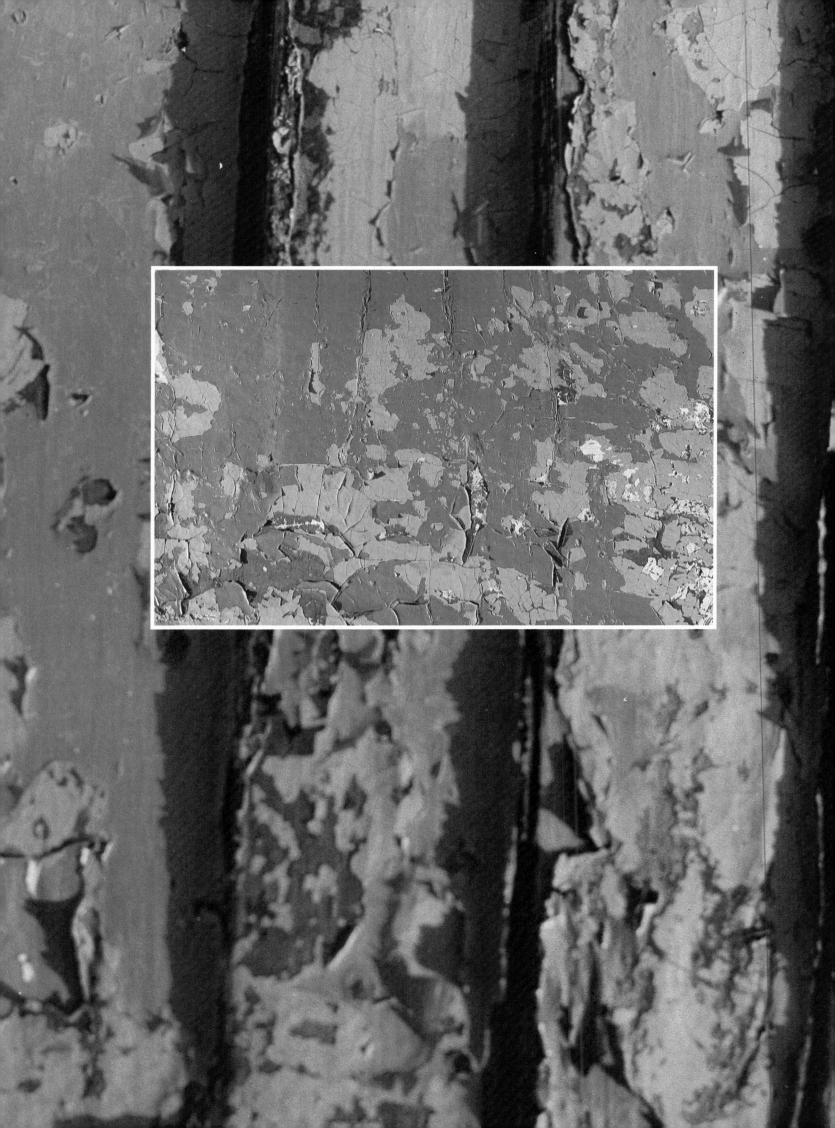

COLOUR

Colour can be the most exciting aspect of any project, but the initial act of choosing a colour scheme is often confusing and worrying. Many people find that although the actual technique of an embroidery might not present any difficulties, deciding which colours go together can!

To help yourself overcome some of these barriers, start by looking at everything around you, to improve your awareness of colour. From time to time, give yourself a subject to observe simply in terms of its colour. You could photograph it, sketch it, or simply take notes. By so doing, you will come to appreciate the number of variations within one colour. For example, over the course of a week, make notes of the types of cloud you can observe from the kitchen window. Clouds are often thought of – and depicted – as simply puffy white blobs or a flat grey ceiling. But they can take many different forms and colours: yellowy-grey before a snowfall, purple-grey before a rainstorm, flecked orange, pink, red and violet at sunset, as well as an unending range of blue, grey-blue, cream, ochre and white for various other weather conditions.

If you are spending time at the seaside, note the changing colours of the sea. A myriad different colours can appear in it – turquoise, violet, light to bottle green, cold grey and glinting silver – depending on the presence of seaweed, rocks, shells and churned-up sand.

Record the effects that the sun, rain, frost,

These close-up photographs of peeling paint on an old boat (opposite) *show a surprising range of colours. Careful examination of such commonplace subjects will often reveal a multitude of hues.*

These studies of leaves (left and above), *made with water-soluble coloured pencils, show the careful rendition of colour variation that comes with close observation. A cardboard frame encloses an area that might serve as material for an embroidery* (see page 46).

The process of abstracting the proportions of colours within a subject is shown in the three examples on these pages. **Right:** the paving around a swimming pool and, **below,** an area of peeling paint, each represented by strips of coloured paper cut from magazines, in widths corresponding to the presence of each colour in the subject.

morning and evening light, summer and winter can make on various surfaces, such as soil, roof tiles and paving, or on a familiar landscape. You may notice, for example, that the bark of a plane tree, when wet, is boldly coloured and patterned, in contrast to its more subdued appearance when dry. The brilliant yellow of rape fields is even more impressive when seen in sunlight with charcoal grey storm clouds gathering behind them. Luminous bluebells are always a delight, but particularly when seen within and against dark green undergrowth.

A heightened awareness of how colours in nature react with each other should help you appreciate the effect that different coloured fabrics and threads will have on each other when combined in a piece of work. Always devote plenty of thought and careful observation to the selection of materials before you begin a project. Remember that 'warm' colours tend to come to the fore and 'cool' ones to recede.

If you are still concerned about combining a variety of hues, choose a limited scheme, perhaps initially working in tones of one colour only. Even within a monochrome range you can give interest to the work by combining warm and cool variations of the basic colour and by incorporating a variety of textures.

Nor must you always use colour naturalistically. You could interpret a mainly green landscape in white, brown or red, if that is your wish. To find unusual or unexpected colour schemes, select small areas of a surface to study. For instance, take a paving stone, a brick wall or a corrugated iron fence. From a distance it may appear grey, red or rust-colour. Make a mental note of that fact. When you observe it close up, however, you will be amazed at the range of colours contained within a small area. List the colours and tonal variations. The paving stone may be primarily sandy grey, ochre and apricot, with small spots of cream, pale grey and brown. The brick, although mainly rusty red, includes a suggestion of grey-lilac, grey-red and tiny flecks of navy blue; whereas the corrugated fence may be sea green, greyish turquoise and mushroom pink, with a flash of apricot orange. Sketch this close-up view, including the various colours; or make a diagram and label the different coloured areas.

The next important step is to note the proportions of the various colours, which is always the secret of transferring a successful colour combination from the original source. Using coloured pencils, crayons or paints, make a sketch of a block of stripes, each stripe representing the relative amount of colour you can see. Alternatively, use coloured papers cut or torn from magazines.

To develop this process a stage further, cut short lengths of fabric and thread and wrap them around a piece of cardboard, trying to match the original colours and their proportions.

Keep a notebook of all your observations. It could soon become an absolute treasury of subtle or sumptuous colour schemes. In time you will find you have discovered a whole range of unexpected colour combinations.

The same method has been used (below) to represent the colours in this photograph of an iris – in this case, using threads, cords and strips of fabric.

The patterns formed by lichen growing on an old statue provided the inspiration for this necktie and matching clutch bag, worked in free machine quilting. The colour values and proportions were first abstracted as described on page 37, in this case by means of strips of coloured paper. The fabric – a medium-weight silk – was then sponged with silk paints in the appropriate colours. After the paints were fixed by ironing in the usual way, the fabric was tacked (basted) to a layer of wadding (very thin for the necktie; slightly thicker for the bag) and a fine backing cloth and quilted freely by machine, using various toning and metallic machine embroidery threads. Tiny beads were added for further textural interest – taking care, in the case of the necktie, to leave the areas to be knotted relatively smooth and flat. An old tie was unpicked to supply the pattern for the necktie. Patterns for clutch bags can be found in craft books; or a pattern can be drawn from an existing bag.

TAKING A THEME

By selecting a subject to study over a period of time – looking at it carefully, then photographing it or sketching it from various angles – you will discover a number of design possibilities within it. A building, a part of your garden, or a rock pool, for example, could provide ideas for a variety of different embroidery projects.

Apply some of the suggestions offered in the previous pages to your study. Try taking one aspect of the image out of its context, making repeat patterns and experimenting with viewpoints, colours and textures. You will find that your first ideas will spark off others. Resist the temptation to assume that you have exhausted the possibilities of a subject. Never be inhibited by the fact that it's been done before. You can always vary the approach to colour, texture, scale and form, or perhaps employ an unusual technique.

Objects can be transformed in various ways to produce more interesting images. Reflections in a distorting window yielded the material for the quilting shown opposite. The still life shown on the next page was given a new dimension with the use of reflective paper below and behind it. The resulting contrast of sharply defined lines and blurred images inspired work in which the shapes relate well to each other and to the background.

The distorted reflections of one building in the windows of another provided interesting thematic material for this piece of machine quilting (opposite). *A section was taken out of context and traced* (left), *then used as a repeating pattern* (below). *The idea was further developed to form a series of variations* (insets, right), *which were rearranged to form the design. Transfer fabric paints (see page 55) were used to print the design on the fabric, and the shapes were outlined with free machine quilting.*

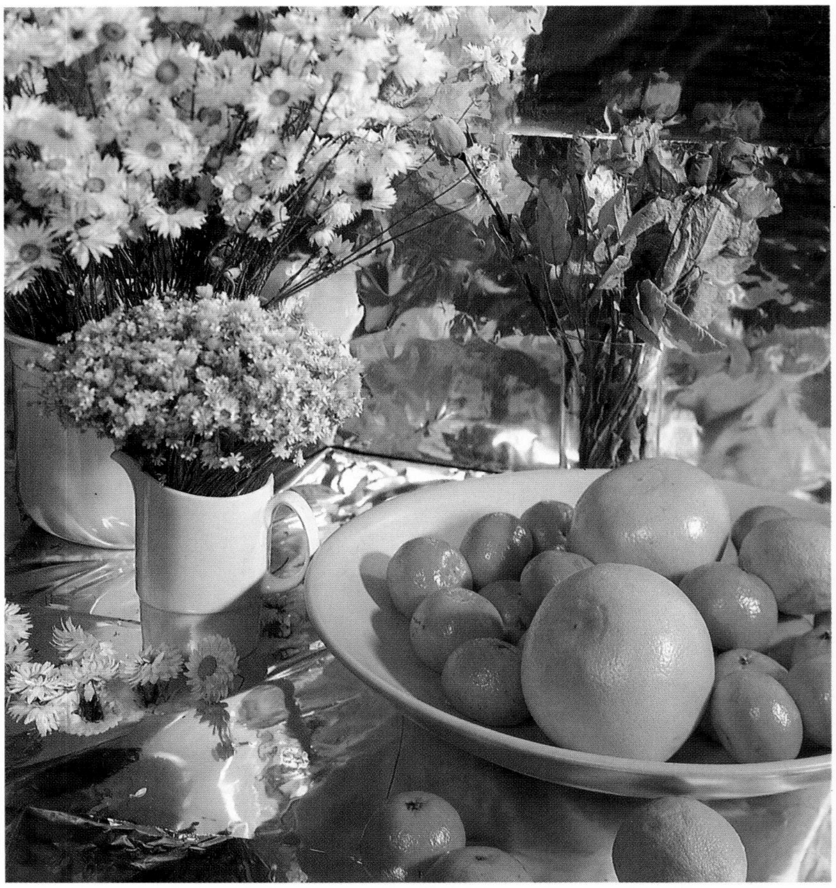

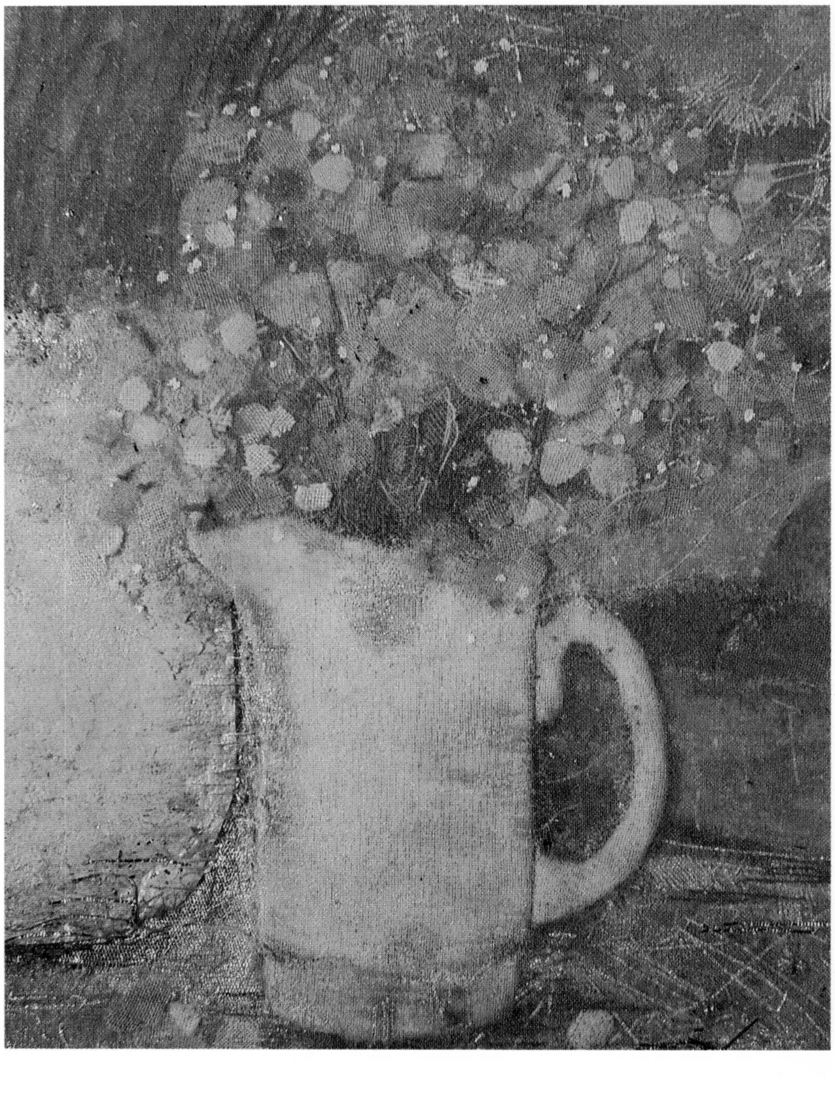

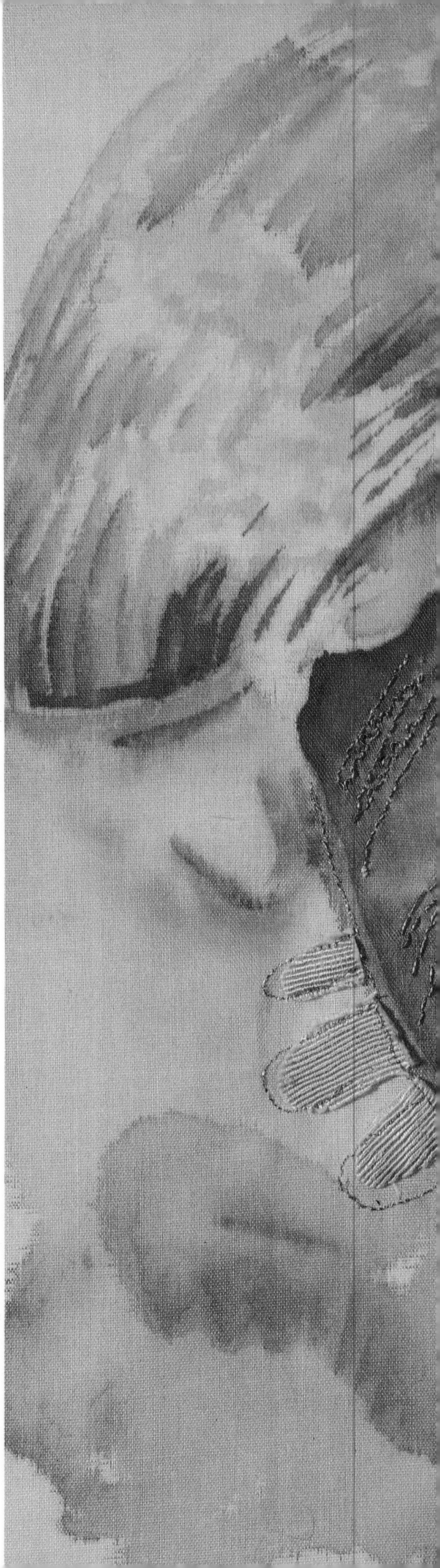

These three embroideries
were all inspired by the
same still life arrangement
of fruit and dried flowers.
The shadow-quilted
picture (far left, below)
was created by applying
the main shapes and small
scraps of fabric and thread
to the background fabric,
then placing a sheer fabric
on top and, finally,
adding more stitchery for
detail. In the main
picture (left) fabric paints
were used to suggest the
main shapes, then the
roses and foil were
accentuated by applying
various fine, sheer and
metallic fabrics; free
machine stitching helped
to define the flower shapes
and reflections. Another
interpretation of the roses
(above) uses small pieces
of painted silk, which were
applied to dissolvable
fabric and outlined and
linked with free
machining; after the
dissolving process, the
result was placed over a
metallic material to
suggest the foil.

43

INTRODUCING FABRIC PAINTS

There is a good range of water-based fabric paints in marvellous colours available these days. They are easy to use at home, are fixed or transferred by ironing and are permanent.

In this section various fabric paints suitable for natural and synthetic fibres are introduced. All of them produce rich and subtle colours. More brilliant hues can be obtained from some manufacturers, but they must be fixed by placing the painted cloth into a special fixing solution supplied with the paints.

No special equipment is required for using the paints described in this section. All you really need is a little space, a tabletop, a board or cloth to protect the surface, an iron and a sink. You may also prefer in some cases to fix the fabric to a rectangular frame to hold it absolutely taut while the paint is applied.

Once you try these paints you will discover how exciting it is to transfer your own designs and colours onto fabric. These uniquely decorated fabrics can then be further embellished with various embroidery techniques.

Interesting effects can be created by applying silk paints freely with a sponge and allowing them to merge with each other, as was done for the fabric and cushions shown here. The upper cushion was machine quilted, the lower one quilted by hand.

SILK PAINTS

Silk paints can be used very easily in your home. They are water-soluble before fixing, so that kitchen surfaces, plates, brushes and your hands can be easily cleaned.

Each fabric paint has its own distinctive qualities. Generally silk paint can be applied to silk, cotton or synthetic fabrics, but it works especially well on pure silk. Because of its fluid consistency, defined shapes cannot be achieved without the use of a thickening agent, available with certain products, or a gutta resist (see page 48). However, the most wonderful effects can be achieved by brushing or sponging the paint onto the fabric; as each colour spreads gently into another, a third colour emerges.

Possible design subjects for this technique include flower gardens and landscapes, especially those with large areas of open fields and sky.

BASIC METHOD

1. Make sure that your fabric is ready to accept the dye. Wash the cloth to remove any dressing or stiffening in it, and iron it to remove all creases.

2. Pin or staple the cloth to a board, or fix it to the work surface with masking tape. If excess paint is used on a horizontal surface, a mini-puddle could form, causing a noticeable edge when the paint dries. (However, this effect can sometimes enhance the design.) Stretching the fabric over a frame or silk-screen can help to prevent the build-up of paint.

This detail of a quilted cushion (below) illustrates the glowing colours that can be achieved with silk paints. The design (based on a section from a brightly coloured leaf – see page 35) was sponged onto a medium-weight silk. The lines were defined with free machine quilting.

The cushions, quilted bag and fabrics shown opposite were all coloured with silk paints. The cushions and turquoise fabric were further embellished by the technique of cut-back appliqué described on page 70. The bag was quilted freely by machine.

3. Pour a little paint onto a plate, palette or bun (cupcake) tin. Mix two or more paints to make new colours and shades, as required.

4. Apply paint to the fabric with a paintbrush (experiment with different sizes), plastic foam or sponge. Colour in the main shapes of your design. Silk paints behave differently on different surfaces. They spread rapidly on silk, less rapidly on other fabrics. Wetting the fabric first eases the flow of the paint but dilutes the colour.

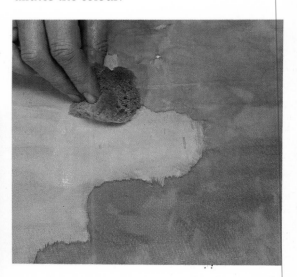

5. Leave the fabric to dry; then iron it to fix the paints. Carefully follow the manufacturer's instructions regarding temperature and method. Most recommend ironing each side of the fabric for several minutes, sometimes with paper or a pressing cloth between the fabric and the iron.

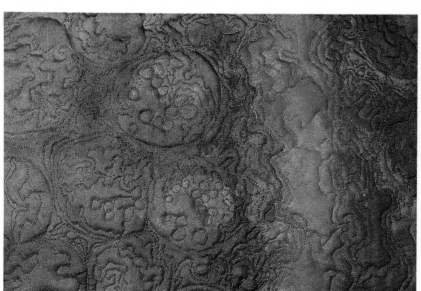

USING GUTTA WITH SILK PAINTS

As you can see from the projects shown on the previous pages, silk paints applied freely to fabric can produce breathtakingly beautiful colours. The merging of one colour into another can be extremely attractive producing all sorts of gradations and subtle patterns.

At times, however, you will want to create more clearly defined patterns on the fabric. One option is to use the permanent fabric paints described on pages 52–53. But if you prefer to use silk paints, with their unique, luminous quality, you can, instead, first outline your design with a gutta resist solution. Then, when this has dried, you apply the colours carefully within the shapes. This method requires a little practice: if you are too heavy-handed or bold with the paint application, the sheer volume of fluid could break down the resist and seep through the broken gutta line. (In some cases, of course, this effect can be used deliberately and most attractively.) Also, handling the gutta itself can be a little tricky at first. But if you persevere, you will discover a wealth of interesting possibilities using this method.

A thin, glue-like substance, gutta is available clear and in a limited range of colours, including gold, silver and black. Coloured gutta lines will remain in the fabric even after washing and must therefore be considered from the outset as part of the design. Clear gutta washes out to give uncoloured areas.

Until recently, gutta came always in plastic bottles equipped with a nozzle. Recently, however, some manufacturers have started selling it in screw-top jars. Unless you are applying the gutta with a brush or sponge, you will need to decant it into a plastic dispenser with a nozzle. This facilitates a fine, even line. An even finer and more easily controlled line can be obtained by fitting the nozzle with a small metal pipette made for this purpose.

Interesting textural effects, such as streaked or stippled patterns, can be achieved by sponging or randomly applying the gutta to the ground fabric.

METHOD OF APPLYING GUTTA

1. Prepare the fabric as for the basic method of applying silk paints, as described on page 46.

2. Tape or pin the fabric to a board, making it as taut as possible. Some people prefer to mount the fabric on a stretcher frame or old picture frame to ensure absolute tautness. This will greatly facilitate painting clearly defined, accurate lines with the gutta and will also help to prevent the paint from forming puddles.

3. Paint the design outlines with gutta, using a fine brush or a plastic dispenser (fitted with a pipette, if desired). Leave the fabric to dry.

4. Flood the paint *gently* into the centre of the motif, allowing the colour to spread out to the resist lines. Leave it to dry. Add more colours as required, in the same way.

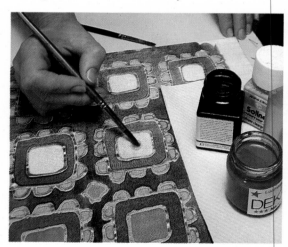

5. Iron the fabric to fix the paint, following the manufacturer's instructions.

6. Hand-wash the fabric gently to remove the gutta. The fabric is now ready to be embellished with your chosen embroidery technique(s).

This little silk bag and matching purse (opposite) were inspired by the shape and markings of a seashell. Silver gutta and metallic fabric paint were used to create the pattern, then grey silk paints were gently applied to the remaining spaces. The fabric was then quilted and made up into the bag and purse.

The design for this silk chiffon evening top was inspired by the colours and textures on a rusty fence. The garment pattern was taken from an existing top, but a commercial dress pattern suitable for soft, fine fabric could be used instead. First, the cream-coloured chiffon was taped to a table protected with plastic sheeting. Then silk paints in the chosen colours were sponged in stripes down the length of the fabric (including the selvedges), allowing the colours to merge with each other. Further paint was added to intensify some tones, and a water-filled sponge was applied to other areas to dilute the colour and create textural water marks. Glitter fabric paint was applied to selected parts of the design. The colours were then fixed by ironing. Finally, running stitches were worked, using a metallic machine embroidery thread, to highlight certain areas of glitter.

The fabric for the evening bag (a silk and cotton blend) was painted with a combination of permanent and silk paints. Gold permanent paint was sponged on in stripes; while it was still wet, black silk paint was applied, allowing the two to intermingle for a soft effect. The fabric was then machine quilted.

PERMANENT FABRIC PAINTS

These fabric paints, like those already described, are easy to use and are unaffected by light, washing or dry-cleaning. They are non-toxic and are fixed by ironing. (The fact that these paints are commonly called 'permanent' does not mean that the silk paints and transfer dyes are not.) You can apply them to any kind of fabric.

All the paints featured in the following pages remain on the cloth exactly as they are printed or painted (unlike silk paints, which tend to spread on the fabric). They can be mixed together to make a wide range of hues. Their relatively thick consistency makes it possible to paint a sharp image on the fabric. Colours can be diluted with water, but do take into consideration the fact that the more fluid the solution is, the less defined the pattern will remain on the material. However, in some cases you may find that a coloured wash can be effectively contrasted with more detailed painting.

In addition to offering a good range of colours, most manufacturers of this type of fabric paint produce fluorescent, pearlized and metallic varieties. (The fluorescent paints are still quite new, and their degree of permanence is not yet established.) Coloured glitter paint is also available; this can look very attractive if some thought is given to how it blends with its background.

BASIC METHOD

1. Wash the cloth to remove any dressing, or finish, which might resist the colour to be applied. Iron the fabric to remove all creases.

2. Cover all working surfaces with newspaper, lining paper or plastic sheeting. Stretch and tape or pin the fabric to a board or the table to make it easier to apply the paint to the fabric.

3. Apply the paint using a brush or one of the other techniques described below.

4. When the paint is dry, iron the fabric to fix the colours. Place a cloth over the ironing board to prevent any dye from marking it, and place the painted fabric right-side-down over it. Always iron the *back* of the cloth, not the front, to fix any of these colours. Use a temperature appropriate for the fabric.

Patterns can be painted onto the fabric with different-sized brushes. Fine, detailed work can be painted with a No. 1 size watercolour brush, larger areas with a 5cm (2in) decorator's brush. The top and sides of the brush can also be used to make unusual marks, and other variations can be achieved by spraying, stippling or dry-brushing the paint onto the cloth. (To dry-brush, use only a little paint, so that the bristle marks will show.)

Sponge is another useful material for printing, and the various densities available can produce different textural effects. Bits of latex foam can be easily adapted to make soft printing blocks. Squares, wedges and strips of foam can be dipped into the fabric paint and printed to form pleasing designs. In most cases the marks produced will be bold, with softly textured edges. You can develop a less

Metallic and plain-coloured fabric paints were applied in a wave pattern to the fabric used for this evening bag (below). The design was accentuated with machine quilting worked in metallic threads.

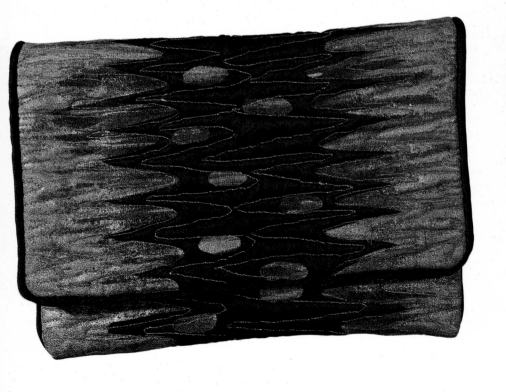

defined pattern by overprinting and over-lapping the shapes. Natural sponge will produce wonderfully irregular textures.

More complex designs can be created by first cutting the foam into more interesting shapes. Draw an outline design on one side of the foam block. Using sharp scissors, cut away the background, leaving a raised pattern. Apply the fabric paint to the block and print it onto the fabric. You can use this technique for carefully placed repeating units or for haphazard arrangements. Other printing materials include potatoes and other vegetables, cork, twigs and leaves.

Masking Techniques

There are several ways of masking the paint from the cloth to achieve interesting decorative effects.

Paper and cardboard templates or stencils can be cut in intricate patterns or torn freely, then placed on the cloth and the paint brushed, sponged or sprayed onto the exposed areas of fabric.

A clear plastic film with adhesive backing is also useful for this purpose. The variety used for covering books is readily available from stationers'. Draw your design on the backing paper, remembering that it will be reversed when printed. Cut out the shape(s) with scissors, or with a craft knife, using a board underneath to protect the table. Stick the plastic film to the fabric, then apply the paint to exposed areas. If necessary the stencil can be lifted carefully from the fabric while the paint is still damp and used again (first wipe the plastic clean with kitchen paper towel).

Simple striped patterns can be developed by placing masking tape of different widths in pleasing arrangements. Make sure that the tape is not lifting up at any point, which might allow the paint to seep beneath it. Unless the fabric is stretched tautly over a frame, some puckering may occur when the colour is applied. This may cause a little variation of colour, but the fabric will regain its shape when dry and ironed.

A mouth diffuser (available from art shops), a spray or an airbrush are alternative ways of applying the colour to the cloth. Obviously an airbrush, used with skill, will produce the most controlled and refined surface.

The stripes produced by the use of masking tape with fabric paints have been further defined (above) *with lines of simple machine quilting.*

This silk scarf (below) was first sponged with yellow and pink silk fabric paint, which was then ironed to fix the colour. Wax was applied and, when dry, cracked quite intensely in some areas. Purple silk paint was then sponged over all the areas to overprint the base colours where the fabric was free of wax.

Wax is a well-known type of resist which can be used with fabric paints and dyes. Specialist craft shops sell refined wax for this purpose. However, for your initial trials, ordinary white household candles can be placed in an old saucepan and melted down over heat into a clear, warm liquid. (For safety, the pan should be no more than one-quarter full. Keep an eye on it, and if it starts to smoke, remove it from the heat.)

WAX RESIST – BASIC METHOD

1. Stretch the fabric as for ordinary painting, and with an old brush apply the wax all over the surface. Alternatively, apply the wax in lines or patterns, only partially covering the cloth. Leave the fabric to dry.

2. Crack the wax in a haphazard way by crumpling the fabric. Slightly more controlled cracking can be achieved by folding or creasing the material in a regular way.

3. Immerse the waxed fabric in a bath of cold-water dye, available from department stores; or sponge silk fabric paint or a diluted permanent paint onto the cracks between the wax. Leave it to dry.

4. Cover a table or ironing board with many layers of newspaper, topped with kitchen paper towel. Spread the cloth on the surface and cover it with another layer of kitchen paper. Apply the iron to the surface; this will gradually melt away the wax and fix the dye at the same time. The paper should soak up the melted wax (you may need to replace it with fresh paper to complete the absorption).

5. When the cloth has regained much of its softness, soak it in some white spirit (mineral spirit) for an hour or two. Rinse and wash it in a solution of mild soap flakes to restore its softness fully.

TRANSFER FABRIC PAINTS

Transfer, or iron on, fabric paints have been designed primarily for use on synthetic fabrics. However, they also give pleasing results on most other fabrics, particularly on cotton and polyester blends. (A colourless solution, manufactured by Pebeo, makes cotton more receptive to the paint.) To use these paints you simply paint your design onto paper, leave it to dry and then transfer it from the paper to the material by ironing it on the wrong side. The print is colourfast and washable. This is an interesting method of decorating a plain fabric, and the resulting design can be further embellished with a number of embroidery techniques.

BASIC METHOD

1. Paint your design onto a smooth, non-absorbent paper such as a fine cartridge (drawing) or typing paper. Dressmaker's graph paper can be used for designs featuring straight lines.

2. Apply the paint to the paper using the appropriate method for the effect you wish to achieve. The illustrations show a range of marks which have been printed, sponged and brushed onto the paper; these textures will be reproduced on the fabric. Remember that the image will be reversed on the fabric, so allow for this at the design stage.

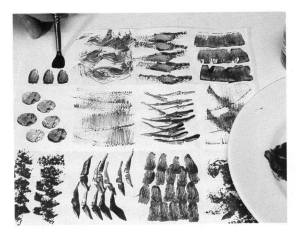

3. Once the painted paper has dried, place the image face down onto the material. Carefully hold or pin the paper to the material to prevent the image from smudging. Set the iron to the temperature recommended by the manufacturer for that fabric. Make sure that the iron has reached the required temperature, then apply it to the paper, moving it gently but firmly over the surface. (Do not allow the iron to stay in one spot, as this could leave an imprint of the iron itself or, if a steam iron, the holes in its surface.) If nylon or another synthetic fabric has been chosen, take care that the iron does not come directly in contact with the fabric, as the fabric could be damaged. Peep under each edge of the paper to make sure that an even and sharply defined design has printed. If the design is still too faint, continue with further ironing.

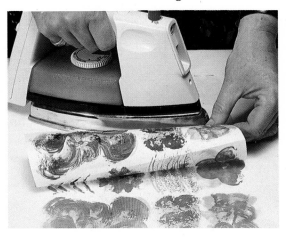

Several images can be printed from one design, but the colours will vary slightly each time. In most cases they will become lighter, although different products vary in this respect. The same paper can be retouched with fresh paint for further printing. The colour will also vary when printed on different materials – nylon, polycotton, rayon, calico (unbleached muslin), and so on; so it is a good idea to test all colours first on a scrap of your chosen fabric. With a little experimentation you will become familiar with the colour variations on different fabrics.

The range of different effects that can be produced by transfer printing the same design onto different fabrics is clearly demonstrated in this example (below) using a motif based on a door. One advantage of the technique, for those who hesitate to draw, is that the design can be traced onto the paper. Also, any false starts can be corrected inexpensively on paper and the design adjusted before it is put onto the fabric.

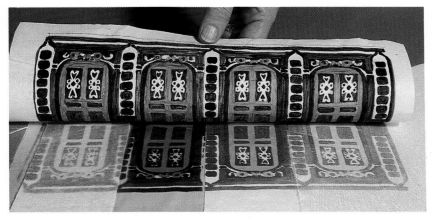

EMBROIDERY TECHNIQUES AND STITCHES

The following section introduces you to some favourite embroidery techniques, both traditional and modern. They will give you an idea of the great range of media available to the embroiderer, each with its own distinctive qualities; and among them you should find plenty of suggestions for interpreting your designs in a sensitive, individual manner.

In years gone by there was a strong emphasis on learning to work embroidery techniques in the approved, traditional manner. Many of these rules were, and still are, useful and well worth learning. But today the emphasis is on free experimentation; if a particular method suits you or produces the effect you have in mind, that is the method to use.

The question of whether or not to use an embroidery frame is a case in point. Some embroiderers use a frame most of the time; others prefer to work without one. You will probably find that some techniques are easier to work on a taut surface, but some are better worked in the hand. When you do wish to use a frame, you have a variety of types from which to choose. Purpose-built rectangular frames can be purchased from specialist embroidery shops and in some department stores. Many people use canvas stretchers. These are available from art shops and consist of strips of wood, made in different lengths, with mitred corners which are slotted together. Some people use empty wooden picture frames. Round tambour frames are usually necessary for machine embroidery.

Before embarking on any sizeable project using a new technique or stitch, do try a small sample first to familiarize yourself with its characteristics. A practice piece should also help you to be more relaxed about trying something new or attempting a larger piece of work.

This profusion of threads and yarns illustrates the wide choice of materials available to the modern embroiderer – a choice paralleled by the range of embroidery techniques, both old and new.

TRANSFERRING DESIGN TO FABRIC

Once you have found or created a design or motif that you really like and decided on a particular technique for its interpretation, you must then transfer your design onto an appropriate fabric. This can be done using one of several different methods.

Paper or cardboard templates These are suitable for simple designs. Pin the template onto the ground fabric (or appliqué fabric), then tack (baste) or mark around the shape with a water-erasable pen.

Photocopies This method is best suited to relatively simple linear designs to be worked on light-coloured fabric (test it first on spare material). Place the photocopy of your design face down onto the cloth and pin it in place. Iron with a moderately hot iron, taking care not to move the paper and blur the image. Remember that the design will be reversed.

A transfer pencil can be used to trace an image on the wrong side of a sheet of tracing paper (below, top) and the image then ironed onto the fabric. If the fabric is sheer, it is possible to trace the image through it (bottom), provided the lines are heavy and clear.

Transfer pencil Using an embroidery transfer pencil, trace your design onto a sheet of paper. Place the tracing face down onto the fabric and iron the design as for a photocopy. If the design is asymmetrical, first trace with an ordinary pencil, then turn the tracing over and go over the lines with the transfer pencil. This will give a correctly oriented image. Note: transfer pencils vary considerably in quality; some are very smudgy and best avoided. Always test the pencil first.

Dressmakers' tracing or carbon paper This is available from most haberdashery (notions) departments and comes in several colours. Place the fabric on a hard surface and position the carbon paper, coloured-side-down, over it. Then pin your design, face upwards, on top. Using a ball-point pen, redraw the design, following the original lines. The shapes will be transferred as designed.

'Prick and pounce' This is a traditional method of transfer and is particularly useful for duplicating a complex pattern. Trace your design onto tracing paper. Turn it wrong side up over a folded towel or blanket. Following the lines and using a medium-sized needle, pierce holes at regular, short intervals. Pin the design, right-side-up, onto the fabric. Roll and stitch a strip of felt into a cylindrical pad. Sprinkle powdered tailors' chalk or talcum powder (originally pounce was powdered cuttlefish) onto the design and gently push it through the holes with the felt. (You will notice that this side is rough, whereas the wrong side is smooth for close contact with the fabric – the reason for first inverting the tracing.) Carefully remove the paper. The design should be revealed as a set of tiny powder dots. Quickly follow this procedure by linking the dots with a water-erasable pen or with a weak solution of white watercolour paint applied with a fine brush. If the fabric is pale in colour, mix a tiny amount of powdered charcoal with the white powder. In this method the design is not reversed.

Trace and tissue paper This method of transfer is suitable for textured fabrics such as velvet or towelling, on which the above methods would not be appropriate. Trace your design onto tissue paper. Mount the fabric on a frame, and pin the paper onto the fabric. Following the pattern lines, tack (baste) small stitches, making sure to fasten on and off very securely. On completion, gently tear away the tissue paper to reveal the transferred image.

Tracing through If you are using a sheer fabric, such as organdy or boiling water-soluble fabric, place the pattern under the cloth and, using a hard pencil or water-erasable pen, trace the design directly. The design is not reversed.

Free drawing If you feel confident and sure of the main lines or shapes of your design, draw directly onto the fabric, using a water-erasable pen, tailors' chalk or fabric paint.

Iron-on transfer paint This is a pleasing method of transferring a coloured image onto cloth (see page 55). Remember that the image is reversed when the design is transferred.

Note that there are a number of air- or water-erasable pens on the market. They work very well on most fabrics, but do try them on the fabric first before embarking on a project.

Remember to pin, tape or weight the design securely to the material, to prevent blurred images and ensure a crisp and precise transfer of the design lines.

PROPORTIONATE ENLARGEMENT

If you have access to a photocopier that has enlarging or reducing capabilities this will provide you with a quick and easy method of altering the size of your design. Alternatively, you can square it up (or down) using the following traditional method. With the help of a ruler, draw a grid on your original design, dividing it into equal-sized squares. Take a piece of paper with the same proportions as the original, but in the required size. Fold or draw a grid containing the same number of squares as the original. Looking at corresponding squares one at a time, draw the same shapes and lines on the bigger (or smaller) sheet of paper.

An episcope (art projector) is a wonderfully useful piece of equipment, although a rather expensive one. Use it to shine your design onto paper taped to a vertical board or wall. Adjust the lens of the machine to fix the image at the desired size, and draw around the projected image. Not only is this a good method of enlarging a design to an appropriate size, but it is an exciting way of observing fine-textured or complex surfaces such as those of leaves, bark, lace and detailed stitchery.

Proportionate enlargement (below) can be achieved by means of an enlarged grid. Compare this result with the distorted enlargement of the same image shown on page 25.

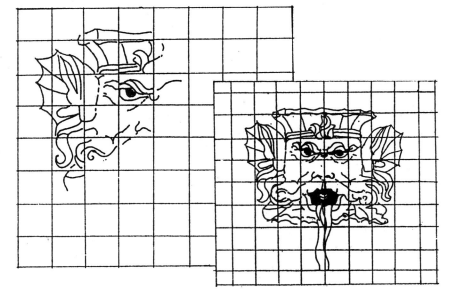

The great versatility of appliqué is suggested in these three examples. Above, a variety of fabrics – sheer, painted silk, net and silver mesh – were applied to a softly painted background fabric, using zigzag stitch, free machining and hand stitches. The geometric design (left) also incorporates silk-painted fabrics (notice the overlapping of the painted shapes), which were freely machine-stitched to a transparent fabric using gold thread. A traditional subject (right) has been given a fresh interpretation; calico (unbleached muslin) and other firm fabrics were first gently coloured with permanent fabric paints to suggest the weathering of an old building. Strips of leather for the window and door frames provide a subtle contrast of texture; and free machine stitching not only holds the shapes in place but gives added definition and pattern to the work.

APPLIQUÉ

When you are considering the technique of appliqué for interpreting a design, give careful thought to your choice of fabrics. If the article is to be worn and laundered, the material should be colourfast, washable and durable. It is usually best to choose similar types of fabric for the shapes to be applied and for the ground material, so that the wearability will be the same and there will be less chance of a puckered surface. In general, you should also match the grain of each appliquéd piece to that of the ground fabric; this, too, will help prevent puckering. Exceptions to this rule might apply if you wish to create certain effects with fraying edges, or with iridescent fabrics.

In the case of purely decorative appliqué, used for creating such items as panels and wall hangings, your choice of fabric is limitless. Wonderful, unusual effects can be achieved by combining corded, textured, rough, smooth, sheer and glittering materials.

The list below includes some of the most useful methods of applying one fabric to another. Each of them has its own distinctive characteristics. The choice of method depends not only on the effect you wish to create and on whether the item is functional or purely decorative, but also on the fabric's fraying tendencies. If you wish to use a fabric that frays easily, but prefer not to turn under the edges, you can apply iron-on interfacing to the wrong side; this will prevent most fraying. The interfaced shape can be applied with small slipstitches if the item is decorative; firmer stitching by hand or machine would be required for functional items. In some cases the textural quality of the cloth can be spoilt by interfacing, so experiment first.

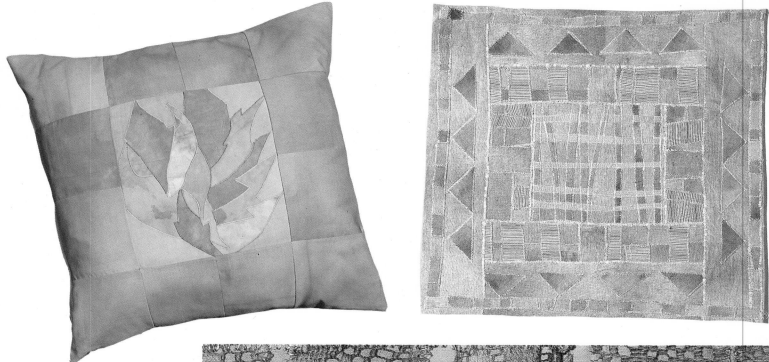

The simple, yet striking, design for this cushion (above) *was achieved by applying the shapes by machine, using close zigzag (satin) stitch. The cotton fabrics were first coloured with silk paints, and the cover assembled using the strip patchwork method.* Above right: *a free interpretation of rectangles and triangles, cut from painted fabrics and applied with free zigzag stitch, which is better suited to this irregular design than the ordinary zigzag used for the cushion. A subtle interplay of colour, shape and texture* (right) *was achieved by applying coloured squares of curtain lace with a wide zigzag stitch to a softly coloured fabric.*

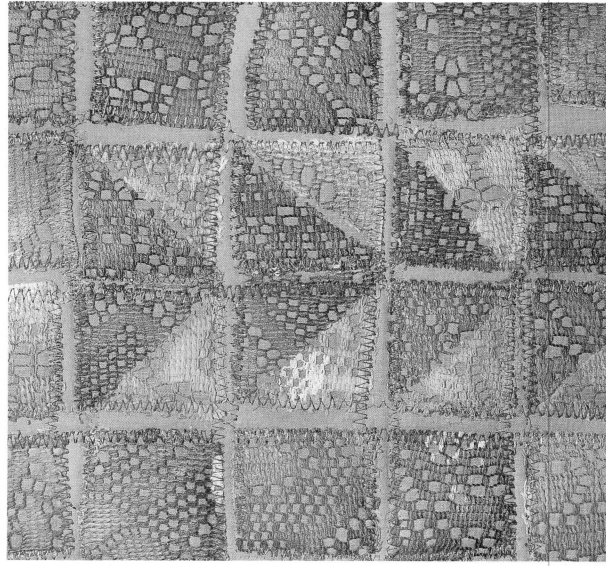

For transferring a design for appliqué, you should make two copies of the design: one for marking the ground fabric, using whichever method seems appropriate (see pages 58–59), and one for cutting up into templates for the appliqué shapes. Mark the right side of each paper template.

Draw around the shapes on the right side of the various fabrics, using water-erasable pen or other suitable marker. If you are using the blind appliqué method, mark a cutting line about 5mm–1cm (¼–⅜ inch) outside the inner line (which marks the finished shape). This edge will be turned under later. Cut out the shapes.

If you wish to work on a frame, mount the ground fabric on a frame of appropriate size, making sure that the grain is straight.

For stitching down the shapes you should normally use a fine matching or toning thread, so that the stitches are inconspicuous and will not conflict with any surface stitchery that you may add at a later stage.

METHODS OF APPLIQUÉ

Hemmed or blind appliqué Carefully turn under the edge on the appliqué shape and tack (baste) it in place. (With experience, you may be able to turn under the edge of most fabrics while applying the shapes.) Curved edges will need to be clipped, so that they will lie flat. Pin, tack (baste) and slipstitch the shape to the ground fabric.

Herringbone-stitched appliqué Pin and tack (baste) the shapes to the ground fabric. Then, using a fine thread, work herringbone stitch over the cut edge. The size and closeness of the stitches will depend on the thickness and fraying qualities of the cloth being applied. Closer stitches are required for easily frayed fabrics.

Machine appliqué Pin and tack (baste) the shapes in place. Then work over the edge by machine, using zigzag or satin stitch (very close zigzag).

Non-fraying fabrics, such as leather and felt, can be applied with small slipstitches or stab stitches (vertically worked running stitch). A little fabric glue will hold the shapes in place for stitching.

Net fabric does not fray, and it can be applied by working tiny stab stitches just within the edge of the shape. In most cases you should choose a thread matching the colour of the ground fabric – not that of the net – in order to make the stitches less obvious.

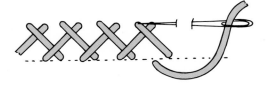

Method of working herringbone stitch

The various methods of applying one fabric to another are illustrated in this sampler (left). The leaf motifs (below) have been applied with close zigzag stitch; notice how the stitch has been gradually narrowed at the points. Straight machine stitching was used to suggest the central vein of each leaf.

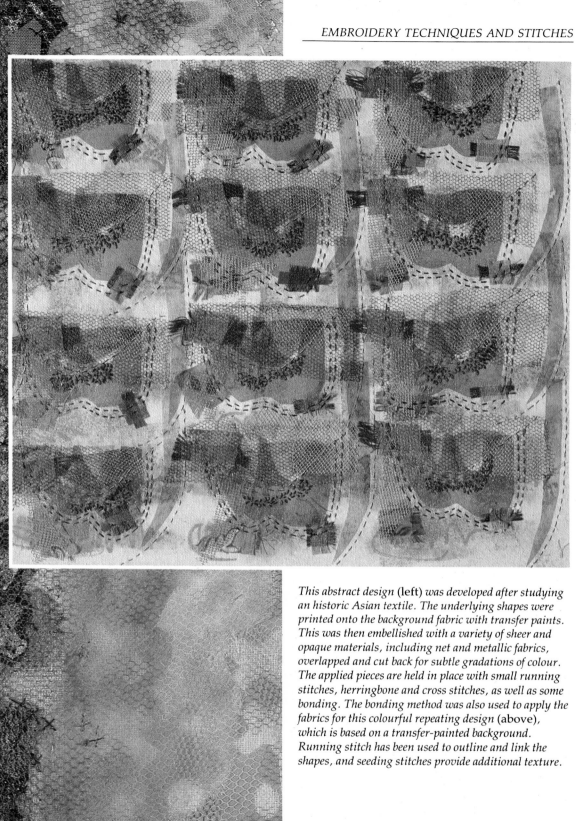

This abstract design (left) was developed after studying an historic Asian textile. The underlying shapes were printed onto the background fabric with transfer paints. This was then embellished with a variety of sheer and opaque materials, including net and metallic fabrics, overlapped and cut back for subtle gradations of colour. The applied pieces are held in place with small running stitches, herringbone and cross stitches, as well as some bonding. The bonding method was also used to apply the fabrics for this colourful repeating design (above), which is based on a transfer-painted background. Running stitch has been used to outline and link the shapes, and seeding stitches provide additional texture.

BONDED APPLIQUÉ

Bonding paper (transfer fusing web) is coated with a fine layer of adhesive and is a convenient means of applying fabrics. First cut out a piece slightly larger than the appliqué shape. Iron the textured (adhesive) side of the paper onto the back of the fabric to be applied. Reverse the template, so that it is wrong-side-up, place it on the paper and draw around it; cut out the shape. Alternatively, the paper can be bonded to the fabric first, and the shape cut through both layers. Peel the paper away from the fabric, and position the shape, glue side down, on the background. Using a damp cloth and a fairly hot iron, press the motif in place.

Bonded appliqué was the technique used for both of these little shoulder bags (below). The silk fabric for the curvilinear design was painted with pink and green silk paints and the colours fixed in the usual way. The shapes were drawn on bonding paper (transfer fusing web) and then cut out and bonded to the fabrics. The shapes were then bonded to black felt and the bag made up. The fabric used for the bag attached to the belt was also coloured with silk fabric paints. The flower motifs were then cut out and bonded to the felt.

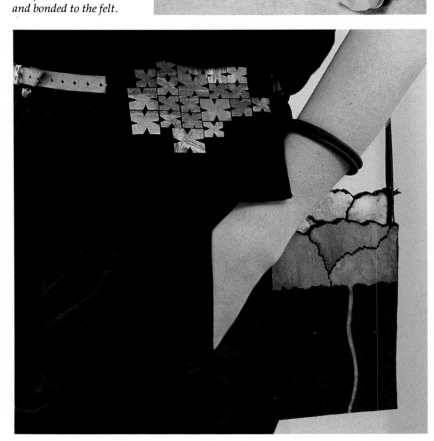

EXPERIMENTING WITH BONDING

You will find experimenting with free bonding wholly stimulating and exhilarating. Original, unexpected and often unrepeatable patterns and textures can be created by this method in a relatively short time.

Instead of backing a piece of fabric with a section of bonding paper (transfer fusing web) and cutting out hard-edged shapes, as described above, you place small pieces of the bonding material on the surface of the ground fabric and cover this with a rich assortment of fabric and thread scraps, which you then cover with sheer material. For the adhesive you can use either bonding paper or ordinary fusible web of the type used for hems. The bonding paper is softer and finer-textured and thus less conspicuous under very sheer fabrics. (A slightly shimmery effect is, however, part of the charm of this technique.) The fusible web is ready to use as is (unlike the bonding paper, which must be separated) and easier to tear; in Britain, however, it is available only in narrow strips.

It is a good idea to begin by experimenting and making a 'texture dictionary', which will allow you the freedom of creating all kinds of effects without having to consider their place in a more resolved piece of work. Later, you can use the technique more selectively, taking into account the appropriateness of certain materials for a fashion accessory, for example, or as an essential part of a panel. Do take care to consider this aspect, so that the finished result does not appear gimmicky.

Using free bonding, you can build up and overlay assorted fragments of muslin, lace and other materials of all types. The richly textured, subtle results can then be further embellished with stitchery on top.

BASIC METHOD

1. Press all materials. If you are using bonding paper, gently pull the adhesive layer away from its backing. If this proves difficult, tear a small amount off one corner, exposing a jagged edge of the adhesive film, which can then easily be pulled away.

2. Tear, or cut, small pieces of the adhesive and position them on the ground fabric where you plan to apply the decorative materials.

3. Place all sorts of interesting snippets on the fabric: tiny fragments of brightly coloured fabrics, threads pulled from cloth, sequins, lace, short lengths of metallic yarn, knitting yarn, silk or ribbons. You may find that you need to add more bonding adhesive between the pieces.

4. Once you have created the textured surface cover it with a layer of natural or pale sheer fabric, such as chiffon or net. Darker colours can also be used, depending on the desired effect. Place a sheet of baking parchment paper on top, and iron everything in place, using a dry iron. The heat will bond the fabrics together to create a type of shadow quilting.

5. Alternatively, you can omit the top fabric, provided you add enough hand or machine stitching to ensure that all the pieces are held firmly in place. Check that an adequate number of adhesive pieces are used and, more importantly, that the surface is well-covered with baking parchment to prevent any of the fragments from sticking to the base of the iron.

Use only a silicone-treated paper, such as baking parchment or the bonding paper backing; other papers, including greaseproof, will adhere to the materials. If you are bonding fragments between two transparent fabrics, cover both the ironing board and the top of the work with the paper to prevent the adhesive from seeping straight through all the materials. For this reason, it is *not* advisable to follow the manufacturer's advice and use a damp cloth when ironing.

These collections of fabric scraps, threads and bits of glitter (below) are the sort of materials that lend themselves to experimental bonding. Because the bonding adhesive stiffens the fabric slightly, it is important always to make a test swatch first to see the finished effect before embarking on a project.

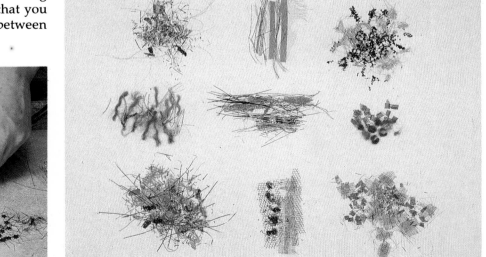

The patterns in rock formations inspired this richly layered piece of experimental bonding (left). Tiny snippets of fabric and thread were placed under sheer and wet-look cotton and synthetic fabrics and bonded in place. Additional texture was provided by free machine stitching in a variety of threads, some metallic. The bow (inset) was also made using the bonding method; two layers of sheer fabric enclose bits of fabric and metallic threads distributed randomly over the first layer and bonded in place using the method described on page 67. The stiffening effect characteristic of this technique is ideal for certain accessories, such as bows and belts. The picture (above) is an interpretation of the still life on page 42. A variety of fabrics were bonded to a background fabric and further decorated with straight stitches worked in silky threads.

CUT-BACK APPLIQUÉ

An interesting variation on the basic appliqué principle is to superimpose several layers of fabric, stitch a design through all the layers, and then cut away one or more layers in selected areas to reveal the fabrics underneath.

The stitching can be worked by hand or by machine, but it must be firm in order to withstand the cutting-away process. Backstitch works well, but make sure to fasten on and off securely. Machine stitching, of course, is even stronger. For a simple motif or grid pattern it can be worked with the presser foot on; less formal designs can be achieved with free machine stitching (see page 77).

When the stitching is completed, cut away the layers as desired, using sharp scissors and cutting as close to the stitching as possible.

For certain kinds of design a more uneven hole may be appropriate. This can be achieved by burning through parts of the fabric before superimposing the layers, using a match. The burning (which works best with synthetics) leaves a singed edge, which will not fray further. Obviously, it is important, when using this method, to observe some safety precautions. Work near a sink or a bowl of water and make sure the room is well ventilated, to diffuse any toxic fumes. Place the fabric on a metal surface such as a draining

Several layers of silk-painted fabric were superimposed for this grid-pattern design (above), then stitched together with lines of close zigzag. Finally, selected squares were cut away to expose the delicate colours. The cushion made from this appliqué is shown on page 47. The pleasingly textured effect of this repeating design (right) was also achieved by the cut-back method — in this case using felt (some coloured with fabric paints) and metallic thread.

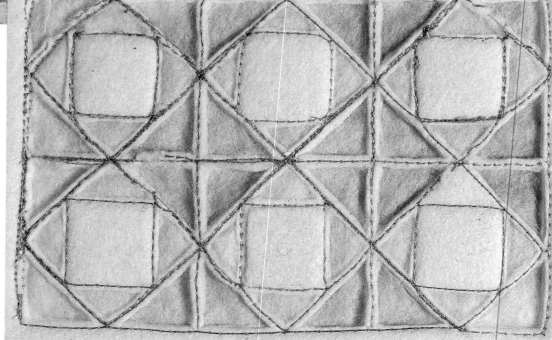

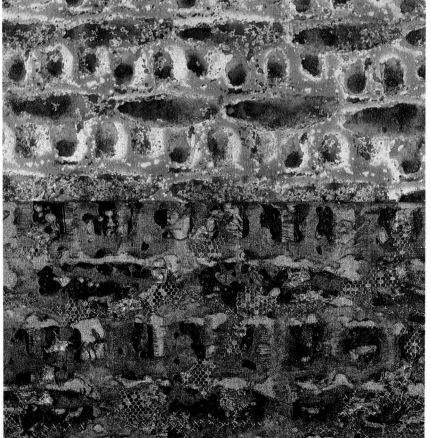

board or old baking sheet and apply the match where appropriate. By experimenting, you will discover the best method of extinguishing the flames on a given fabric – in water, or by smothering them with an old oven glove.

When using this method, make sure that it is appropriate for the surface you are trying to create; otherwise it could appear gimmicky.

The circular pattern of this subtly coloured fabric (above) *was worked freely in straight machine stitch, using metallic thread, through several layers of net and sheer fabrics. Then layers were cut away to produce the interesting colour variations, and the fabric used to make the drawstring bag* (inset). *The same method, using a rose colour scheme, was employed for the fabric of the clutch bag. This experimental piece* (left) *is an interpretation of an ink and bleach design, using layers of synthetic fabric burned away in places to expose the ground fabric. Small pieces of metallic net and other fabric have been used to embellish the surface.*

71

DARNING

The pictorial and textural possibilities of darning are illustrated (opposite) *in these four examples of the technique. Clockwise, from upper left:* trees, *worked in surface darning;* tulips, *darned in a variety of matt and shiny yarns on curtain mesh; an abstract design worked partly into the ground fabric and partly in surface darning; and a simple diamond pattern darned in a variety of threads.*

This simple landscape (below) *was worked in vertical and horizontal darning and running stitch on a painted fabric. Below, right:* a *rich assortment of materials, including shiny threads, metallic knitting tape and chenille yarn, have been used to create this attractive texture.*

The term 'darning' immediately suggests the mundane occupation of mending. But don't be put off by this prosaic image; for this easily worked technique can produce quite distinctive, even stunning effects.

Simple horizontal darning consists of working straight running stitches over and under the threads of the ground fabric, sometimes varying the length of the stitch and, thus, the number of ground threads covered. For your first venture, choose a fabric in which the threads are easily counted. It should have a relatively open weave, which will remain undistorted by the darning. Choose a variety of threads, both matt and shiny, approximately the same thickness as the fabric threads. If you wish to include a thicker or textured yarn, you may need to withdraw some of the threads from the ground cloth to accommodate them. A good starting exercise would be to make a simple design of stripes, possibly including fabric strips or ribbons.

Pattern darning is a popular form of decoration throughout the world, and charming abstract and figurative patterns can be produced by systematically varying the length of the stitches across the cloth. Each line worked will gradually build up the pattern. Intricate designs can be worked out first on graph paper, letting each line of the printed grid represent a thread of the ground fabric.

A freer approach to darning can produce more original results. Drawings and observations taken from your sketchbook, photograph albums or magazines could be simply and effectively interpreted. Choose a subject that has strong vertical and/or horizontal lines – nothing too 'busy'. Some suitable starting points could be landscapes featuring horizontal bands of fields, crops, hedgerows or clumps of trees in the distance. A beach with breakers rolling in towards the shore would make an ideal subject, with interesting possibilities for contrasting different texture of thread. Skies often have wonderfully subtle horizontal cloud patterns.

Plants, trees and scenes viewed through railings would be more effectively suggested in vertical darning. Subjects with a high degree of textural interest, such as weather-eroded rocks, stone carvings, or lichen-covered old walls, could inspire a three-dimensional use of the technique, working the darning in layers.

The characteristics of the ground fabric will have a strong influence on the finished work. You might use an evenweave linen (one having the same number of threads per centimetre [inch] in warp and weft), scrim, sheer curtain fabric, a vegetable bag or rug canvas (first soaked in water to make it more pliable).

Various landscapes served as inspiration for this beautiful screen (below; detail right), which is worked entirely in darning. The main shapes were initially blocked in with horizontal darning; then areas of vertical darning were added for textural interest.

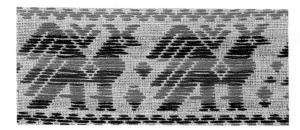

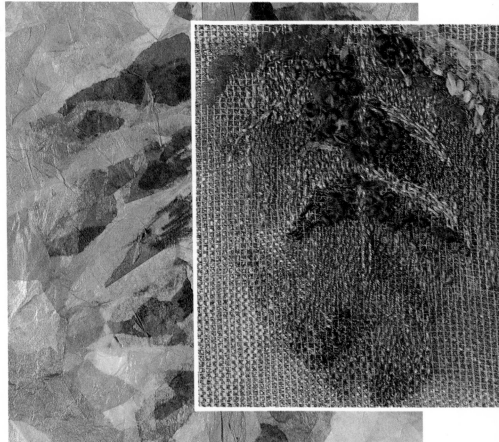

Curtain nets (open-weave curtain fabrics) are ideal for darning and come in a wide range of grid sizes. The colour range available may be limited to white and cream; but you can dye it to suit your purpose. Silver, gold and iridescent mesh can be purchased from some department stores and from shops specializing in theatrical fabrics.

Threads used for darning should normally be compatible in weight with the background fabric. However, you can withdraw threads from the ground fabric if necessary to accommodate thick or highly textured ones.

The technique itself is easy to do, but before you begin the project do give some thought to the range of yarns and the spacing of the threads to be darned in. This freer approach can develop images in all sorts of directions. Layers of texture can be built up by surface darning. This is worked by laying additional ground threads on top of the first layer of darning and then darning in more threads to achieve the required effect. You need not always darn in straight lines; gentle, flowing movements can be darned, so long as the lines are not too exaggerated in angle and thus distort the cloth in an unattractive way.

FREE-DARNING – BASIC METHOD

1. Tack (baste) the lines of the design, or mark them with water-erasable pen. If the fabric is loosely woven, you can place the design underneath and trace through the main shapes. Alternatively, you can colour or block in the pattern with fabric paints. This treatment will also help blend the colours of the thread to the ground material.

2. Another method is to devise the pattern on graph paper, and then use this as a guide for working the darning.

3. Thread a tapestry (blunt-pointed) needle or bodkin with the chosen thread. Fasten on (and off) by darning into the back of the work.

4. Work the stitches smoothly, taking care not to distort the fabric.

5. If some of the threads are thicker than those of the ground fabric, withdraw fabric threads,

Above, left: this charming example of Mexican pattern darning decorates the yoke of a child's dress. The leaf markings (above), composed of cut and torn tissue paper, have been interpreted in darning, using a wonderful variety of threads. The ground fabric of this striking design (left) was first coloured with fabric paints, then darned with wool yarns.

if necessary, to accommodate them.

If you wish the image to be bolder, continue working layers on top of certain sections. Further interest can be achieved by adding vertical darning over the horizontal threads.

MACHINE EMBROIDERY

Many people think of machine embroidery in terms of the automatic patterns that can be produced by some machines. But the really interesting machine work is created by embroiderers using the machine freely to exploit the possibilities of ordinary straight and zigzag stitch. This technique offers a marvellous range of effects, but sadly many people feel that it is beyond their capabilities. You really can succeed, given a little time to practice free machining before undertaking any large objects.

Although some very old sewing machines can be adapted for embroidery, a model that will do zigzag stitch (sometimes called a swing-needle machine) is the type to use. These days most machines have this facility. With a little practice you will be surprised how easy it is to create very competent images, and you will soon become aware of the variety of decorative lines and textures you can use to embellish your work.

Initially, learn to 'draw' with the machine. Using a straight stitch, make abstract doodles of loops, circles, waves, leaves and cross-hatching to familiarize yourself with the feel of the machine. Follow this by drawing a simple design on the fabric – perhaps a few flowers and leaves, a tree or a simple landscape. To provide a guide for the stitching, you might quickly sponge some fabric paint onto the fabric (see pages 46–53), indicating areas of flower and leaf or field and sky. As well as giving you a general guide for the stitching, the colour will disguise any hesitant, wobbly lines that may occur. As a general rule, choose threads slightly lighter in tone than your instinctive choice in order to ensure a successful blending one with another and prevent harsh lines.

Begin by outlining the main shapes, and follow this by blocking in other areas with solid stitching. Zigzag stitch can be used effectively, and quickly, for this purpose. A combination of linear patterns and contrasting areas of solid stitching often makes the most successful design.

'Normandy Remembered' (opposite), by Jean Littlejohn, is a distillation of images drawn from the cathedrals of Bayeux and Rouen, using a combination of techniques and materials: permanent fabric paints (some metallic); applied sheer fabrics, including muslin, scrim, net and lace; and a delicate tracery of hand and machine stitching.

The main features of this little landscape (left) were blocked in with fabric paints. Bits of net were applied in places, using free machine stitching, both straight and zigzag, which gives additional texture. The ground fabric of the geometric design (below) is a rug canvas, sprayed with metallic paint. Shaded fabrics, including bits of lace curtain, have been applied to the canvas and embellished with free machining using metallic threads.

BASIC METHOD

1. It is advisable to read your machine manual and set the machine for darning. Few manuals mention embroidery unless referring to the set patterns. Thread the machine as usual. Initially, any ordinary sewing thread will do; a fine size 50 is recommended. At a later stage you will probably be tempted to try some of the wonderfully coloured and textured machine embroidery threads which are now available.

2. A size 80 or 90 needle is generally sturdy enough for machine embroidery, although a coarser needle may sometimes be necessary. Do not worry if you break a few needles; it happens to everyone at some stage or another.

3. For free straight stitching, make sure that the stitch width and length dials on the machine are set at 'O'.

4. Remove the presser foot and, following your manual's instructions, lower or cover the feed dog (teeth). This will enable you to move the fabric in any direction, rather than just forwards and backwards.

5. Select a narrow, round (tambour) frame, measuring about 20 cm (8 inches) in diameter, with an adjustable screw. It is a good idea to bind the inner ring with woven tape to ensure a tight grip of the fabric. Adjust the outer ring so that it fits comfortably, but not loosely, over the inner ring. Place the fabric (a smooth, medium-weight cotton is best) over the inner ring and press the outer one over it. The fabric should be extremely taut; loosely framed fabric encourages uneven stitching and broken threads. If the fabric is not drum-taut, remove the outer ring, tighten the screw and repeat. Make sure that the fabric grain is straight.

6. Put the frame under the needle with the material flat against the machine top, or bed, so that you stitch into the well of the frame (the opposite of hand stitching).

7. Put down the presser foot take-up lever; this engages the tension. This is an essential step, and it is so easy to forget to do if there is no foot in place. Most machines are equipped with a darning foot, which some people like to use for machine embroidery because it keeps the material flat under the needle, helping to ensure uninterrupted machining. However, it does obscure a tiny area of the work (unless it is made of clear plastic) – a disadvantage when working intricate designs.

8. Before you start stitching, move the balance wheel (hand-wheel) to take the needle into the fabric and bring up the bobbin thread.

9. Hold the frame firmly but in a relaxed way, as shown, and start to stitch. Make a few stitches to fasten on, then snip off excess threads. Move the frame easily and smoothly in all directions, trying to keep a steady, constant speed. Make lots of doodles, followed by petal, flower and leaf shapes; you might also try to write a word. The speed at which you move the frame determines the stitch length. The faster you move it, the longer the stitch. Practise until you feel more relaxed. Try not to hold your breath, and don't go too slowly! Working in one place will tend to break the thread. Enjoy the freedom and – compared to hand stitchery – the speed of the stitching.

As already suggested, you might go on to create a small flower garden picture. Using fabric paints, brush or sponge on areas of colour, then leave them to dry and fix them by ironing (see pages 46–53). Thread your machine in the appropriate colour, and mount the fabric in a frame. Work details of the design in machine stitching. Do not try to depict each flower, but just suggest an overall effect. Once you have become familiar with the basic technique and character of machine embroidery, you can use it to interpret your own original design ideas. Some people find working with a frame inhibiting, and many embroiderers work with a backing material called Stitch 'n' Tear to support and stiffen the ground fabric, which is pinned or tacked (basted) to it. In this case a darning foot is also used to keep the cloth as taut and firm as possible. When the embroidery is completed the backing is torn away.

PROBLEMS IN MACHINE EMBROIDERY

Everyone encounters the occasional problem in machine embroidery, such as missed stitches or broken threads. In dealing with such problems you may find the following suggestions helpful,

• The fabric may be too loose in the frame. Remount it, making sure it is absolutely taut. Also try using a darning foot.

• You may be moving the frame too erratically. Jerky movements can break threads.

• You may be running the machine too fast or too slowly.

• You may be forgetting to put down the take-up lever.

• Your needle may be blunt or be placed the wrong way around.

• Fluff or fibres may be caught in or around the bobbin.

Some of the new silky and specialist threads run through too quickly and shred or tangle around the spool. In most cases this can be rectified by:

• Taping an ordinary sewing needle to the top of the machine and including it in the threading-up process to steady the speed of the thread. Some manufacturers supply an accessory that can be fitted to the existing spool to achieve the same result.

• Using the silky thread in the bobbin and a matching sewing thread on the spool and working the embroidery wrong-side-up.

• Using a larger needle. Some thread manufacturers specifically recommend a size 90 needle with certain threads.

• Altering the top tension. Refer to the machine's manual for instructions.

'Spring, Summer and Lilac Skies' (above) *incorporates machine stitching and appliqué on water-soluble fabrics, as well as some hand stitchery.*

A selection (left) *of multi-shaded, silk and metallic threads for machine embroidery. Beautiful effects can be achieved with these threads, so enjoy experimenting with them. Binding the ring frame with cotton tape, as shown, will help to keep the fabric taut while stitching.*

The stages involved in creating a piece of machine openwork and appliqué on a water-soluble fabric are shown at **right**. A part of the snapshot at lower left was used for the design, shown in the sketch. Above, two flower motifs, worked on the soluble fabric over the traced lines. Note that the lines have been re-stitched several times and that all lines link up; this is most important. At right, appliqué motifs to be incorporated in the work and, below, the finished embroidery.

The daisy bag (**below**) was created using mainly the method illustrated above; some of the flowers were worked separately. The earrings (**below, right**) were inspired by strawberry flowers and worked on water-soluble fabric.

MACHINE OPENWORK ON WATER-SOLUBLE FABRICS

Exciting lacy textures can be created on your sewing machine, thanks to the new water-soluble, or dissolvable, fabrics. You first adjust the machine for free embroidery (see page 78), then work the embroidery in the same way, using the dissolvable cloth instead of an ordinary one. When the embroidery is complete you immerse the work in water to dissolve the fabric.

The resulting lacy fabric can be used in all sorts of ways: for earrings and other accessories, to embellish clothing and household linens and as appliqué motifs and layers of texture on decorative embroideries.

POINTS TO REMEMBER

• Machine your design lines several times over to make quite a heavy line. Use a straight stitch initially, even if it is to be covered with zigzag stitch. Worked on its own, zigzag stitch unravels when the ground fabric is dissolved, unless it has been very heavily layered.
• Make sure that all the shapes connect with each other, or your design will fall to pieces when you dissolve the backing fabric. Before doing so, hold the work up against a light to check this.

BOILING WATER-SOLUBLE FABRIC

This is a fine, pale blue, closely woven fabric.

1. Work the embroidery. When the design is complete, cut away the excess fabric from around the edges.

2. Plunge the work into boiling water. The fabric will dissolve immediately, and the work will shrink up into a small shape.

3. Take the embroidery out of the water and rinse it in cold water.

4. Stretch it out to the correct shape over a folded towel, pin it into shape and leave it to dry. For a flat texture, iron the work.

As this process produces a stiffish finish, the work can also be modelled while wet and will retain its shape when dry. For a softer finish, re-immerse it in the boiling water; the more plunges, the softer the finished result. Some threads will shrink, so experiment first.

This piece of machine embroidery, worked on water-soluble fabric and shown along with the sketch that served as the design, shows the subtle, lacy effects that can be achieved using this method.

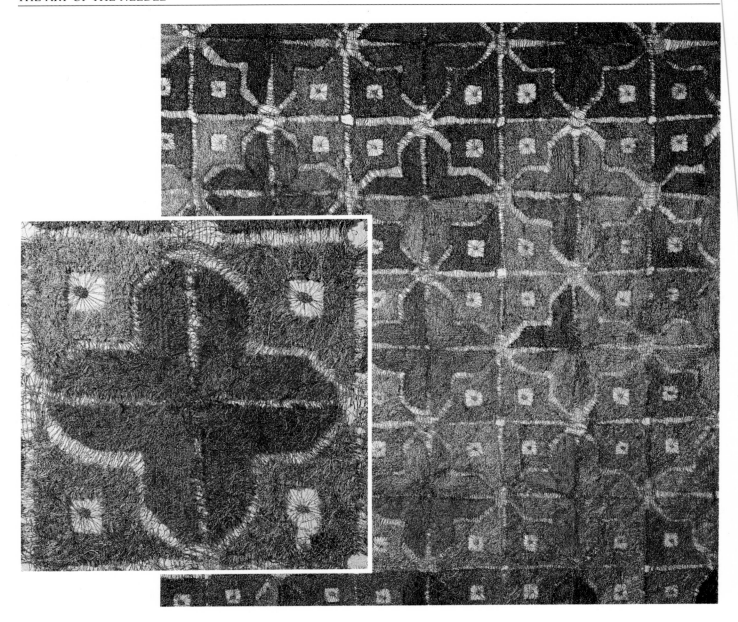

*'Tegel Quadrangle'
(above, with detail), by
Karen Fleming, was
created by densely
machine stitching a
variety of rayon and
metallic threads on water-
soluble fabric.*

COLD WATER-SOLUBLE FABRIC

This is a colourless plastic type of fabric. Do not sneeze or spill water on it, as it dissolves very quickly!

1. Machine the design as usual, making sure to link all the stitching lines. (You might find that you need to use a finer needle and a couple of layers of plastic in the frame to prevent tearing.) Cut away the excess fabric.

2. Place the embroidery in a bowl of cold water to dissolve the fabric.

3. Block or press the work, as appropriate.

This is an easier method than the first, but the fabric is not quite so nice to work on, especially if your preference is layered and textured embroidery. The result has a softer finish, unless metallic threads have been used; these will give it some stiffness – as, of course, will appliqué motifs cut from firm fabrics.

Scraps of either fabric can be patched and machine stitched together and used for further work.

Appliqué shapes can be incorporated in both techniques. The boiling-water cloth withstands a warm iron, so light bonding can be carried out; whereas the cold-water plastic will melt with the heat. Pin or tack (baste) appliqué pieces to the dissolvable fabric in the conventional way, then machine them in place as desired.

Each method has its advantages and disadvantages, and in time you will prefer to use one rather than the other. As you can see from the illustrations, quite splendid effects can be created.

OTHER MACHINE OPENWORK TECHNIQUES

Another lacy effect can be achieved by machining onto vanishing muslin. Here again, it is important to connect all design lines. When the stitching is completed, iron the work at the temperature specified for cotton, or place it in a moderate oven for about six minutes. The muslin will gradually crumble away. However, this technique is quite time-consuming and gives variable results.

Machine cutwork is another way of creating lacy effects. In this technique you first cut holes in the fabric and then work free machining around and across the holes. Alternatively, you can rearrange and distort the fibres of a loosely woven fabric into a pleasing pattern, and then stitch freely over them. Remember to keep the fabric taut in the frame; the use of the darning foot will help to ensure smooth machining.

Machine openwork can be used to create many interesting accessories. The sample (above) is made of shapes freely machined onto water-soluble fabric. The bowls (below) combine the technique with that of moulded paper pulp, which was used to form the basic shapes, over plastic bowls, and then dyed and left to dry. The lacy centre and surface decoration were stitched on water-soluble fabric, moulded while still wet and strengthened with PVA glue, which is transparent when dry.

PATCHWORK

Patchwork is a much-loved traditional technique. There are many different ways of piecing together small fabric shapes to form a larger pattern, and new approaches to this timeless craft are continually being devised.

For best results, all fabrics used for the patchwork should be of the same weight and fibre content. The traditional rule is to match the sewing thread to the chosen material: cotton thread with cotton fabric, silk with silk and synthetic with synthetic. Modern cotton-covered polyester is suitable for most fabrics, but silk thread should still be used for sewing on silk.

With easy-to-use fabric paints you can create the most wonderful colour schemes using a white or natural-coloured fabric of your choice and colouring it as desired. The days of searching for a particular colour in a suitable fabric are over!

HEXAGON PATCHWORK

In this enduringly popular type of patchwork solid-colour and/or patterned fabrics are cut in hexagon shapes, which are then joined to form an attractive arrangement. To give this method a new character, try using smaller templates than the size usually recommended and fabric that you have dyed or painted (see pages 46–55) in your own colour scheme.

BASIC METHOD

1. Use a purchased metal or plastic template; these are widely available in a variety of sizes. (If you wish to use extra-small hexagons, tape a template to a piece of paper and make a reduced photocopy of it. Use this as a pattern to cut a sturdy cardboard template.) Draw around the template on stiff paper to make the required number of shapes.

2. Cut out the paper shapes, taking care to be as accurate as possible.

3. Pin the paper shapes to the material, matching the grain with one of the straight edges. Cut out each fabric shape, leaving a 5mm (¼ inch) border for turning.

4. Carefully turn the edges of cloth over the paper shape and tack (baste) them in place. Prepare a number of patches in this way before beginning to assemble the patchwork. It is sometimes helpful to arrange the patches in the desired pattern and pin them to a sheet of polystyrene (Styrofoam) or a pinboard; this will ensure that they are joined correctly.

5. Place two patches together with right sides facing, lining up the edges accurately, and oversew the edges with tiny stitches in a fine matching or toning thread. Using this method, sew all the patches together. Half or partial hexagon shapes may have to be made to fill out the edges of the complete shape.

6. Take out the tacking, and press the work, if necessary, before removing the papers. Do not iron the patches with the tacking in place, as the stitch indentations may remain.

This sampler (below) illustrates the stages involved in constructing a piece of hexagon patchwork. The two cushions (opposite) show how this traditional method can be given a fresh interpretation through the use of fabric paints. The top cushion, made of silk fabric, was based on sweet peas; the other, made of cotton, on fading hydrangea blooms. Silk paints, plus a little pearl permanent paint, were used to produce the soft colours.

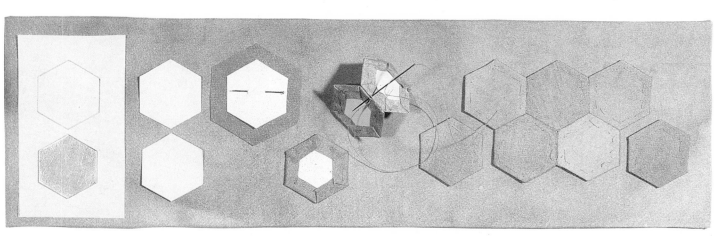

LOG CABIN PATCHWORK

This sample of log cabin (below) is based on a square measuring 7.5 cm (3 inches), with strips of fabric about 2.5 cm (1 inch) wide. A medium-weight silk fabric, coloured with silk fabric paints, was used for the sample. It is fairly easy to gauge the positioning of the strips so that they cover the foundation square accurately; however, some people prefer to work out the design on graph paper.

This popular form of patchwork is an easy and effective way of using up small pieces of fabric. Patterns are made from overlapping folded strips of fabric, stitched in sequence to a foundation square around a small centre square of material. When several squares have been completed, they are then pieced together to form a larger unit. Traditionally, square units often measures 30 cm (12 inches) for a quilt or perhaps 10 cm (4 inches) or 15 cm (6 inches) for a cushion. Worked in smaller units, this technique can look even more effective.

One traditional log cabin pattern uses tonal variations: light colours on two adjacent sides of a square, with darker colours on the re-

maining two. Different effects are obtained by arranging the light and dark areas in different ways. Getting the desired tonal variation can be tricky if you are limited to commercially dyed and printed fabrics; but if you dye the fabric yourself (see pages 46–53) you can get attractive results relatively easily.

BASIC METHOD

1. Decide on the size of the square and cut the required number from a backing fabric, such as mull or a lightweight calico (unbleached muslin). Mark each square with a diagonal cross to establish the centre, using tacking (basting) or a water-soluble pen.

2. For the centre square cut a piece from the chosen fabric, making this about one-fourth to one-third the size of the backing square. Position this in the centre of the marked square and sew it in place with running stitches or by machine, about 5 mm (¼ inch) from the edge.

3. Cut lengths of fabric on the straight grain, making them three times the width of the finished strip and as long as feasible; they will be cut to fit as you go. Turn under one-third of the width along one edge and press. (Some people prefer to place and stitch the strips before pressing, as described below.)

4. Take one of the strips and cut off a piece the same length as one edge of the centre square. Place it right-side-down along the edge of the square, raw edges matching, and sew it in place along the crease. If you have not pre-pressed the strip, position and cut it in the same way, then stitch about one-third in from the edge; fold the fabric back to expose the right side, and press.

5. For the next strip, place the length along the second side of the square (working clockwise), and cut a piece measuring the same as the centre square plus the width of the first applied strip. Stitch it in place as before. Continue to sew the strips around the centre square as shown, overlapping the raw edges of the previously applied strips by one-half (one-third of the original width) each time.

6. When all the single units have been completed, join two squares by placing the right sides together and machine stitching along one edge. Join all the squares one to another, endeavouring to keep the seams straight, with the corners of each unit meeting exactly.

SIMPLE STRIP PATCHWORK

There are many approaches to creating unusual patchwork. Some of the most stunning effects can be achieved by the simple technique of joining fabric pieces together to make strips and then joining the strips to form a design based on squares, stripes or a chevron pattern. Alternatively, the same method can be used more freely to make a type of 'crazy' patchwork of assorted shapes forming an attractive mosaic of pastel hues or vibrant colours.

The example shown on this page and the following page was made from calico (unbleached muslin), subtly coloured with silk fabric paints. Several random shapes were cut from the fabric, with extra allowed for seams, and moved around into a pleasing arrangement. The pieces were machine stitched together to form a strip. A variety of patched lengths were then joined together with additional pieces fitted in to complete the design.

BASIC METHOD

1. Press all fabrics before beginning the work.

2. Decide on the width of the first strip, and cut out appropriately sized fabric pieces, including a seam allowance of about 1 cm (³⁄₈ inch). You could cut square or rectangular pieces or a mixture of both. You could also include diamond shapes, adding right-angled triangles at the corners to complete the square or rectangle.

3. Begin by placing two fabric pieces together with right sides facing. Pin, tack (baste) and machine along one edge. Continue joining the shapes one to another, following this method, to form a strip of assorted pieces.

4. After you have made several of these strips, join them in the same way on their long edges to form a large piece of patchwork. If the strips are of uneven length, extra patches can be slotted in to regularize the overall shape and size as required.

If you would prefer to create a complex or very precise design, in which absolute accuracy is essential, you could first plan the work in detail on graph paper and then cut out the appropriate templates, adding a standard seam allowance throughout. A narrow masking tape, available from quilters' suppliers, can be used on the edges of each fabric shape to help guide your

stitching and to ensure regular seaming.

An interesting variation on strip patchwork can be achieved by sewing the patches together with open seams. Tack (baste) the shapes onto water-soluble fabric (see page 81), leaving a small gap between them. Then stitch back and forth to join the shapes, and dissolve the fabric in the usual way.

But even using the ordinary strip patchwork method you can create exciting fabrics very easily, without being overwhelmed by a mass of technical points. However, you may wish to attempt a more ambitious project, in which case you should consult some of the specialist books on patchwork for further guidance on design and technique.

The wrong side (below) of the patchwork shown on page 88 shows the method of constructing strip patchwork and is an interesting surface in its own right.

Overleaf: the right side of the work – a wonderfully subtle arrangement of pieces cut from silk-painted calico (unbleached muslin). The patchwork forms the cover of a large floor cushion.

QUILTING

English, or wadded, quilting is a very popular, attractive and easy embroidery technique. Basically it consists of making a 'sandwich' of two fabrics with a layer of padding in between and then stitching these layers together in a decorative pattern.

The stitching can be worked by hand or machine. Especially attractive results can be achieved using the free machine quilting method described below, which enables you to stitch in any direction.

The bottom layer, or lining, can be mull, muslin, soft calico (unbleached muslin), or even an old sheet. The middle section is called wadding (batting) and is available in several varieties. Polyester wadding is easy to obtain from local shops and quilters' suppliers. In Britain (where it is often called by the trade name Terylene), it is commonly available in two-, four- and eight-ounce weights, indicating increasing order of thickness. In the United States most batting sold corresponds roughly to the British two-ounce weight, although thicker, 'high loft' varieties are also available. Cotton batting (usually with a small percentage of polyester to prevent the cotton fibres from 'migrating') is also widely available in the US; and wool batting can be bought from some shops and mail-order companies. In Britain, cotton domette is a possible alternative to polyester wadding if a relatively flat texture is required. An important thing to remember when choosing wadding is that the

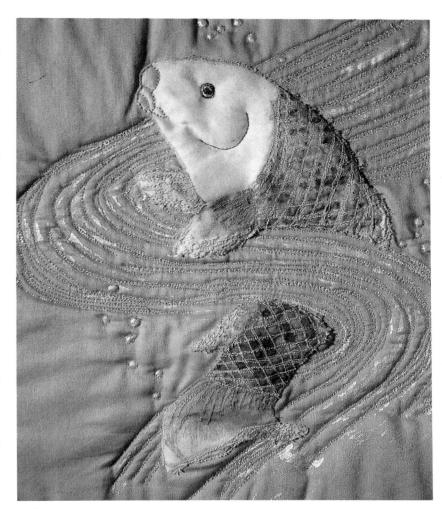

thickness after quilting will usually be about half of the original thickness of the wadding. Two or more layers of wadding can be used to obtain the necessary thickness in the finished work if a suitable weight is not available.

The top fabric can be of any type, so long as it is firm or fairly tightly woven, so that the weave does not separate in an unattractive manner when stitched. Shiny fabrics are often most effective, because they reflect light and thus enhance the contrast between the raised areas and the stitching.

The thread used for the stitching should be strong and, usually, of the same fibre as the top fabric. Special quilting thread, made of cotton-wrapped polyester, is a good choice for most purposes. Silk buttonhole twist (if you can find it) is ideal if you wish to make a feature of the stitching itself. To ensure that the three layers of fabric are firmly held together, an allover design is generally considered the most suitable.

This fish motif (above) – one of several on a quilt – was transfer-printed onto a piece of polyester-cotton fabric, then quilted freely by machine, using various machine embroidery threads. The pretty little cushion (left), featuring heart motifs, is made from a medium-weight silk, coloured with silk, pearlized and metallic fabric paints. Running stitch was used for the concentric lines and the heart motifs; the edging was worked by machine.

Method of working backstitch

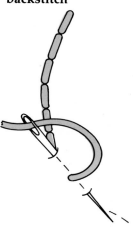

This example of hand quilting (below and, right, in progress) is worked in backstitch. The design, based on the reflections shown on page 40, was transfer-printed onto the fabric.

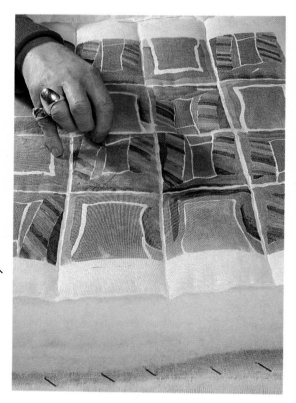

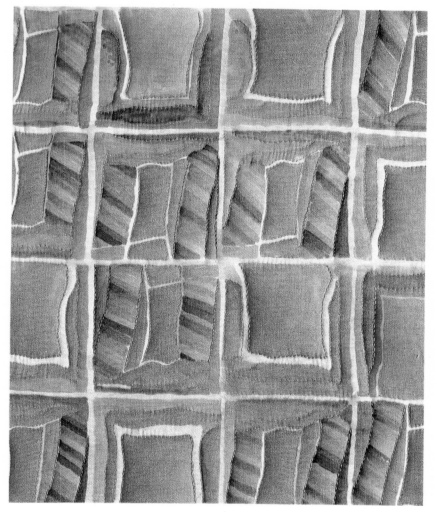

BASIC METHOD – HAND QUILTING

1. Cut the three fabrics to the required size, allowing a generous margin on all edges to allow for 'shrinkage' during the stitching; the thicker the wadding, the more shrinkage will occur. It is a good idea to include an extra margin along one side of the design, to be used for some practice stitching before each work session. Even experienced embroiderers find that it takes a while to build up a smooth rhythm of stitching, and this practice will ensure even stitches in the finished work.

2. Transfer your design onto the top fabric (see pages 58–59, using the most appropriate method. For a simple design, the template method may be most suitable; for more complex ones, dressmakers' carbon or the prick-and-pounce method may be the best choice.

3. Mount the lining fabric onto a rectangular frame. A stretcher frame, or old picture frame, is fine for small projects; secure the fabric to it with drawing pins (thumb tacks). Large projects, such as quilts are generally worked on a special quilting frame; instructions for mounting the work on such a frame are normally supplied by the manufacturer. Make sure that the grain of the fabric is straight and runs at right angles to the sides of the frame. Pin the wadding and top fabric to the lining. Beginning at the centre and working outwards, to eliminate uneven areas of padding, tack (baste) the fabrics together, making a grid of horizontal and vertical lines.

4. Again starting from a central part of the work, stitch along the lines of the design. Use a single strand of thread, of a length you find comfortable, and fasten it on the underside of the work with a knot or a couple of backstitches. For a clearly defined line of stitching, backstitch (shown above, left) is the best choice. It is easiest to work the stitch in two movements, stabbing through the layers of fabric. The evenness of the stitches is more important than making them tiny.

For relatively flat projects, such as traditional quilts, running stitch is often used. If you are working on a quilting frame, which leaves the fabric slightly slack, the stitch can be worked with a sewing movement. Again, however, strive to keep the stitches even.

For making up articles such as bags and cushions, which entail joining pieces with seams, you will need to trim away any excess wadding up to the seamline, taking care not to cut the top or lining fabric. Then continue with the normal making-up procedure.

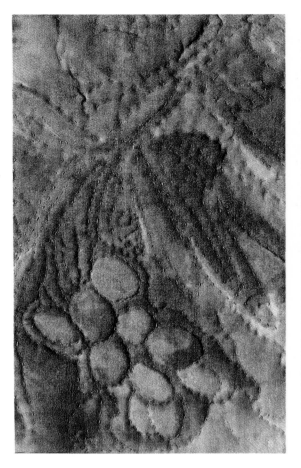

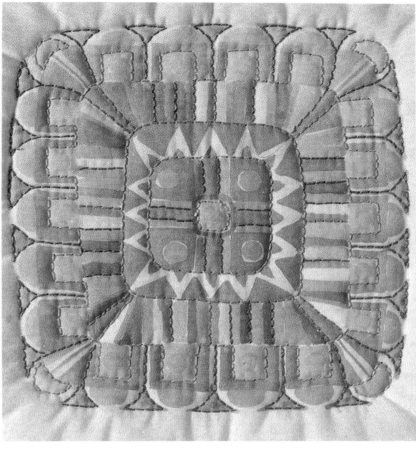

BASIC METHOD – FREE MACHINE QUILTING

Very simple designs can be quilted by machine with the presser foot attached as for normal machine stitching (see illustration, page 53). However, for more intricate designs you will need to work as described below.

1. Prepare the layers of fabric and padding as for hand quilting, but do not mount the work on a frame.

2. Set the machine for free stitching or darning (see page 78). You will probably find that a darning foot (shown in the photograph at right) will help to keep the fabric firmly in place and enable you to produce smooth and even stitches.

3. Thread the machine with the appropriate threads. Do consider using some of the varied machine threads which are now available. Shaded and metallic yarns can give unexpected and attractive results.

4. Place the fabric under the needle, lower the take-up lever, and work a few stitches to fasten on. Holding the work firmly in your hands and stretching it at tautly as you can, machine your design lines freely in any direc-

tion. It is a good idea to begin at the centre of the design and work outwards to prevent misplaced 'bumps' of padding.

The surface can be further enhanced by the addition of handstitching to emphasize parts of the design.

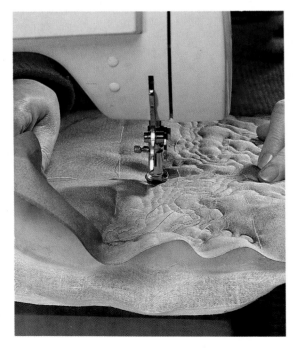

Transfer printing was also used to apply the designs for these two pieces of quilting. The fruit and foliage design (above, left) is worked in running stitch; the square motif (above, right) was inspired by a border pattern on a decorative collar in a museum and was quilted using backstitch. Several of these motifs were joined to form a cot quilt.

SHADOW QUILTING

Shadow quilting is an extremely attractive and delicate technique, well-suited to fine household linens, such as tablecloths, to lingerie and to purely decorative items such as pictures and greeting cards. It consists of a simple pattern of brightly coloured fabrics and/or threads positioned between two layers of semi-transparent fabric and stitched in place so that they show through in a shadowy way.

Any transparent or sheer fabric, such as organdy, organza, lawn, voile or chiffon, is suitable. When choosing a material, test its translucent quality by placing a postage stamp or similar finely detailed image beneath it to see how clearly it shows through.

Designs for shadow quilting can be developed in various ways. A border to decorate a tablecloth, sheer curtain or window blind (shade) might be created using a cut paper pattern. A suitable motif for this purpose could be adapted from an object found around the house, a green plant, a section taken out of context from a photograph of a building, or a decorative object in a museum. If you are planning a picture or greeting card in shadow quilting, you might use a flower garden, a market, a landscape or a seascape as the basis of your design.

If the design will be made of identical fabric

Shadow quilting has been used (right) *to create this pretty interpretation of the still life shown on page 42. The image has been further embellished with small pieces of fabric applied over the top layer.* Above, right: *an assortment of ribbons shadow quilted between two layers of cotton voile, using straight machine stitch.*

shapes, as for a border pattern, make cardboard templates and trace around these to ensure uniform shapes. Freer designs can be built up by cutting out fabric pieces and positioning them on the background, perhaps with the design underneath as a guide.

BASIC METHOD

1. Cut out the shapes that will form the design from the chosen fabrics.

2. Arrange these pieces on the bottom layer, holding them in place temporarily with pins or permanently with bonding (see page 66) or a dab of fabric glue.

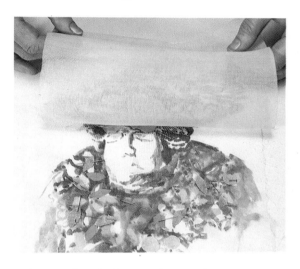

3. Pin and tack (baste) the top fabric in place (first removing any pins from the bottom layer).

4. Choose a suitable thread which tones with or complements the design and the chosen fabric, then backstitch or machine stitch carefully around the shapes. Use running stitch for a less defined line. The process of stitching the layers of fabric together increases the clearness of the image. Avoid using too dark or bright a thread for the stitching, as this will tend to detract from the subtle effect desirable in shadow quilting. If parts of the design need lifting or accentuating, this can be done with added surface stitchery.

Remember to choose fabrics, threads or ribbons that are colourfast if the item is to be washed. However, if you are making a purely decorative piece, you can have great fun experimenting with beads, sequins, seeds, novelty threads, lace or different coloured felts, sandwiched between the fabrics.

Especially attractive designs can be created by first transfer printing the image onto an opaque background fabric, using the method described on page 55. This not only serves as a guide for placing the pieces of fabric but also gives exra depth to the design. Position the snippets of fabric, threads and other materials, cover them with the top fabric, and quilt in the usual way. The sheer top layer could also be transfer printed to echo and/or accentuate elements of the design formed by the quilting. In this case, take care to keep the colours on the top fabric soft, so that they will not overpower the shadowy image.

Of course, other kinds of fabric paint can also be used and combined within the same piece of work. A block-printed metallic paint glinting through the sheer top layer could be most effective.

Still another variation of the technique is to pad the design from the underside, as in trapunto quilting. In this method you first stitch the design through the two main layers of fabric, using machine stitch or backstitch. Then snip the bottom layer where appropriate and insert bits of yarn, dyed wadding (batting), or other materials through the hole. Finally, close the opening by hand.

'Auntie Esther' (above) illustrates the use of transfer paints to block in the image, which was then built up with a variety of materials to suggest dress fabrics and hat trimmings. White organdy was used for the top layer, and pastel threads for the backstitching. A little seeding was used for accents.

Shadow work techniques were used for both the blouse and the tablecloth shown here. The bluebell motif used for the tablecloth is the one given as a border pattern on page 17 and used for the circular cloth on page 19. After being enlarged to the desired size, the leaves and flowers were traced onto cardboard; the resulting templates were then used to trace the shapes onto bonding paper (transfer fusing web). The un-cut tracings were then fused to the wrong side of the chosen fabrics, and the shapes were cut out. The shapes were bonded to the main fabric, a piece of polyester voile, as described on page 66 (after first placing baking parchment beneath and on top of the work – a necessary protection for board and iron when bonding sheer fabrics). Another layer of voile was placed on top, and lines of backstitch were worked around the shapes to accentuate them and hold the layers of fabric together. The edges were finished with a narrow binding made from a strip of the voile.

Two layers of synthetic organdy were used for the shadow-quilted blouse (detail above), but in this case the periwinkle motifs were printed onto one layer of the fabric using transfer paints. The second layer of fabric was placed on top, and two or three lines of free machine stitching were used to outline the flower shapes. The top layer was then carefully cut away between the flower shapes. Finally, the blouse was cut out and made up.

95

EMBROIDERY STITCHES

'Reflections' (detail, below) by Jane Clarke, a small panel worked entirely in freely placed cross stitches of different sizes, using a variety of threads and ribbon, demonstrates the exciting effects that can be achieved by working stitches in unconventional ways. Another embroidery worked entirely in cross stitch, 'Clematis' (opposite), by Jean Littlejohn, employs delicately coloured chiffon fabrics, interspersed with smaller stitches worked in embroidery threads to build up a richly varied texture.

If you are fascinated and attracted by exciting colours and textures, then you will certainly enjoy experimenting with surface stitchery. Although neat, regular rows of stitching are still applicable today and are absolutely the correct embellishment for certain items, changing attitudes now encourage you to experiment with stitches and work them in unconventional ways. You will discover that unique textural effects can be achieved, and that these, in turn, will be a source of inspiration for other projects.

Start by collecting a variety of different coloured threads. You will find yarns with wonderful textures. They can be thin, thick, matt, shiny, rough, smooth, multicoloured, shaded, metallic, stranded, twisted, slubbed, wrapped, hairy, looped, and so on. Look for oddments of weaving, knitting or crochet yarns, as well as those manufactured specifically for embroidery. Working with long strips of fabric, old nylon stockings, woven tapes, ribbons, and strings can also result in unusual effects.

Choose a ground fabric that will suit the style of work intended. For instance, if you are aiming to create a heavily stitched and textured piece, use a strong fabric such as hessian (burlap) or a furnishing fabric, which will take the weight of the stitchery without puckering. For finer work a smooth cloth such as lightweight linen is suitable. Mount the fabric on a wooden frame if you like to stitch into a taut surface. Or you might prefer to work with the fabric loose in your hand and then damp-stretch the piece after it is completed (see page 120) to eliminate creasing.

Select a needle with an eye the right size for the chosen thread. Crewel needles are suitable, as are chenille needles, which have relatively larger eyes and come in a greater range of sizes. (Size 10 chenilles are sometimes sold as 'heavy embroidery needles'.) At times you may wish to use an extra large needle or stiletto to pierce a hole in the ground fabric so that a thicker thread can be eased through. Start and finish your stitching with a double stitch or by darning into the back of the work.

Experiment with one stitch. Work it in many types of thread: a smooth, matt yarn will clearly show the structure of the stitch, a fraying strip of fabric or woolly yarn will make an interesting texture and not show the stitch so clearly defined. Vary the size or scale of the stitch; work it in many directions, crosshatching or building it up in layers. Work it in a diagonal, vertical, circular or haphazard way, depending on the surface you are interpreting. Remember that thick, dense stitches will result in strong tones of the thread colour, and sparse, thin ones will give a paler effect.

Try breaking some of the old traditional rules of stitching. Enjoy the immense pleasure of creating unique stitched surfaces. For far too long, some approaches to conventional stitching have been inhibiting, so make the stitches work for you.

There are hundreds of embroidery stitches, but some are considerably more useful than others. The stitches chosen for this book are among the most popular with professional embroiderers and students alike. They are relatively easy to work and extremely versatile, lending themselves to an enormous variety of effects.

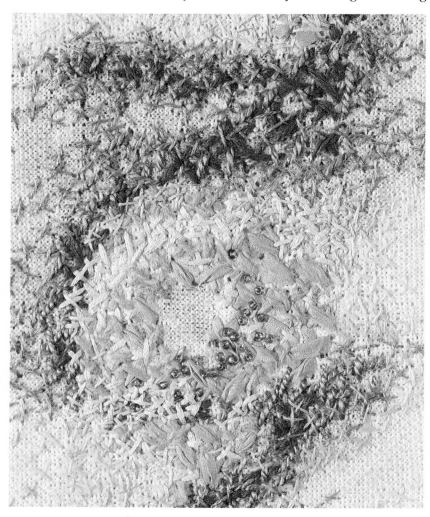

BUTTONHOLE STITCH

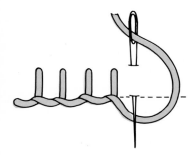

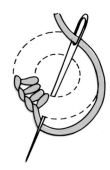

**Two methods
of working
buttonhole stitch**

This is another stitch that offers many alternatives. When the stitches are worked very closely together, the result is usually referred to as buttonhole; when worked in a more open arrangement, they produce the familiar blanket stitch.

Always be ready to experiment with a stitch in the hope of creating a new pattern or texture. By overlapping or layering lines of buttonhole stitches, you could achieve an effect suggesting rock strata or undergrowth. By working it in circular movements you could suggest flowers or barnacle-encrusted surfaces. The centre of the circle could be open or closed. The scope is limitless.

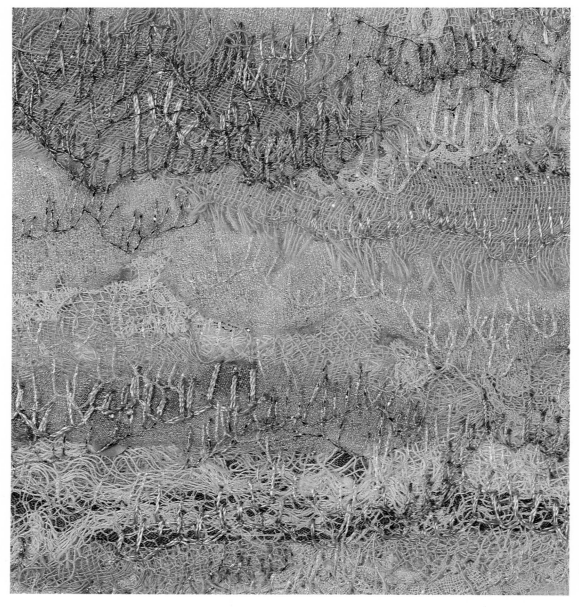

This attractive design, suggestive of rock strata (right), was worked in a variety of matt, shiny and metallic threads and shows how effective buttonhole stitch looks when worked in encroaching lines. The sample (above, right), shows buttonhole stitch worked in circles.

CHAIN STITCH

This stitch looks pleasing when worked formally and conventionally, and in this form it can be found decorating many historical and ethnic pieces. It can also be most exciting when sewn with uneven spacing, looped or layered as illustrated, and offers tremendous scope for the creative embroiderer. For example, the ridges and indentations on a piece of tree bark might be interpreted in lines of chain stitches, some of which could be superimposed to give a three-dimensional effect.

Detached chain stitches, which are perhaps most familiar worked in a circle to make 'lazy daisy' motifs, can be used as fillings or overlaid to suggest the textural qualities of a wall, a flowerbed, pebbles on a beach or the foliage of a tree. Try working the stitch in thin strips of fabric or woven tape, putting one stitch inside the chain of another, or highlighting a stitch with a bead.

Twisted chain is a simple variation of the basic chain stitch which produces an attractively textured line. Try working it in a range of different threads.

Varieties of chain stitch: detached chain (a and b), ordinary chain (c), twisted chain (d and e), raised chain band worked in a line (f) and freely, as a filling (g).

Raised chain band is a particularly useful variation of chain stitch. Worked conventionally, it forms a line; however, it can also be used to form areas of texture. First work a row of parallel bar stitches; then work chain stitch over these bars, without working into the fabric. All sorts of different effects can be created by, for example, varying the length and spacing of the bars and working the bars and the chain stitch in contrasting colours. Close bars and fine thread produce a 'knitted' texture; more widely spaced bars and firm threads show the chain stitches more clearly.

This sampler (below) shows chain stitch worked in a variety of threads and approaches. Top row; left to right: ordinary chain worked conventionally, with varied spacing and superimposed; middle row: detached chain stitches used to build up different textures; bottom row: lines of twisted chain stitch.

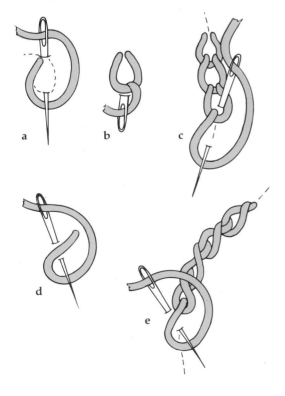

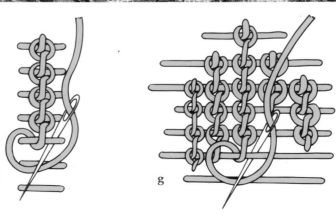

Opposite, left: *This charming interpretation of a flower garden was worked entirely in raised chain band, using a great variety of threads. The other two photographs (opposite, right) show the process of building up a rich texture in this stitch. Notice that some of the chain stitches pass over a bar; this helps to give a fluid quality to the work. The completed sample (right) of raised chain band has a dense, highly tactile surface.*

Overleaf: *The wonderfully textured and coloured outer and inner surfaces of an abalone shell, together with their interpretations in embroidery. The heavily encrusted exterior is suggested by dense lines of raised chain band; the iridescent interior by waves of glossy couched threads on shiny fabric.*

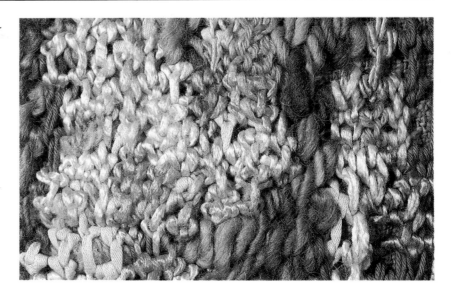

COUCHING

Couching is a very useful stitch to know. It can be worked in a single line, to define a pattern clearly; or a number of lines can be massed together, perhaps using a variety of threads, to make a solid area of texture. It is particularly useful when you wish to incorporate threads that are too thick, highly textured or delicate to be pulled through the fabric, as in other stitches. The thread is placed on top of the fabric and held in place with stitches worked in an ordinary thread; only the starting and finishing ends of the couched thread are taken to the wrong side, where they are secured with a couple of stitches in the finer thread. If the fabric is firmly woven and the couched thread very thick, use a stiletto to pierce a hole through which to pull the thread.

wrong side with a few stitches in the finer thread. Place the main thread in the chosen position and sew it down, with the finer ·thread forming straight stitches across it at regular intervals. Keep the main yarn taut for best results, unless you want to produce a loose, loopy effect. The more intricate, linear or geometric the arrangement, the closer the holding-down stitches will need to be. As a general rule, these should be inconspicuous, so that they do not compete with the pattern made by the main thread. However, the holding-down thread can be stitched in a more obvious way, perhaps in strong diagonals, if counter-rhythms are needed for the required effect.

Graceful lines of couching (below) have been enlivened by looping other yarns and threads over the couched threads. This stitch is excellent for depicting flowing movement.

Thread two needles: one with the main thread, which should be relatively thick, and the other with a finer toning thread. Begin by easing the thicker yarn through from the back of the fabric and securing the end on the

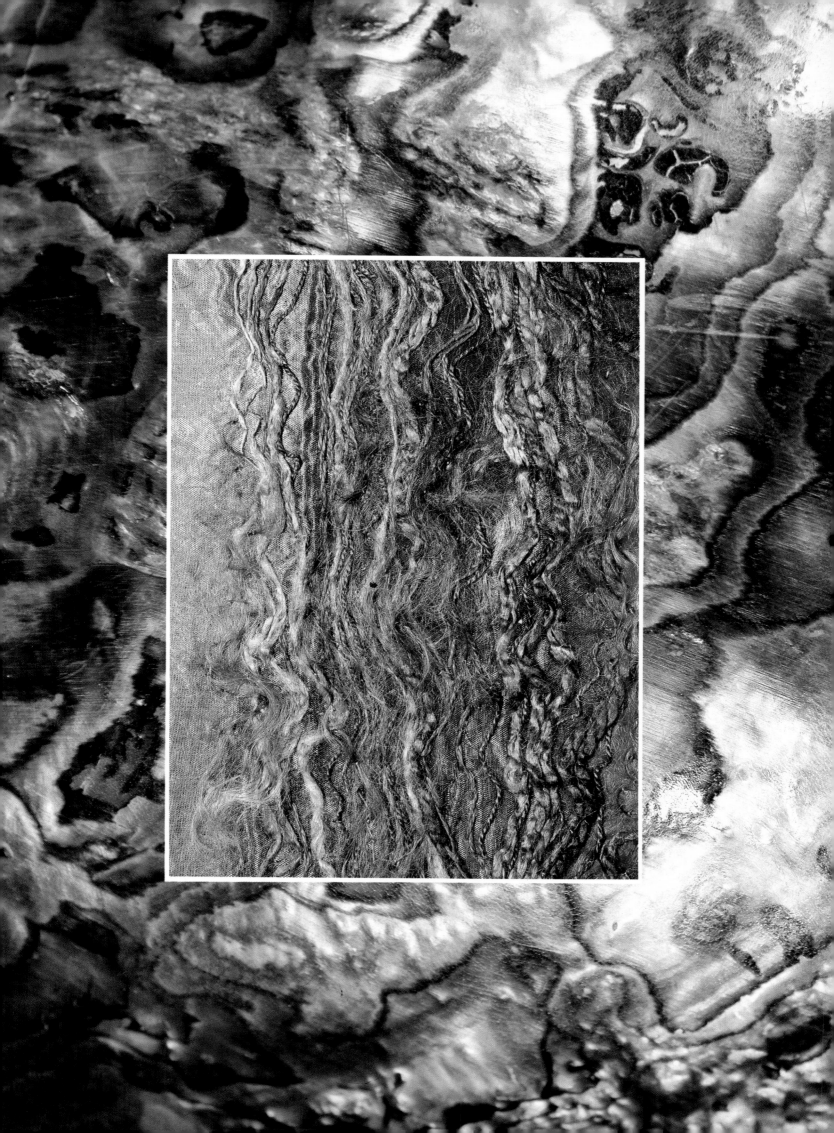

CRETAN STITCH

This is another favourite stitch. You will be continually surprised at just how many variations you can achieve with it. Try working the stitch in a wide range of yarns, stitching it in undulating or encroaching lines; these could be used to depict fields of grain or grass or certain kinds of foliage. By turning the work sideways and working the stitch vertically as usual, you can produce attractive horizontal lines, suggestive of ripples or reflections in water, or cloud patterns in a sky. Another possibility is to work the stitch in a circular arrangement to represent floral or star patterns. Beads can also be incorporated while working the stitches. Cretan stitch is particularly useful for blending colours.

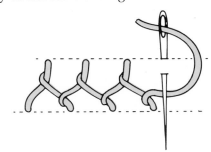

The main colour areas of this design (right) *were blocked in with fabric paints; then Cretan stitch was worked in varying directions, giving the surface an attractively spiky quality. The incorporation of a few glass beads in some stitches gives additional textural interest. The fascinating interplay of soft colours and textures in lichen on an old slate tile* (opposite) *has been interpreted* (inset) *in closely massed Cretan stitch, worked mainly in fine threads such as* coton perlé. *The more heavily textured areas of lichen have been suggested by using thicker threads, including wools, and by layering stitches on top of one another.*

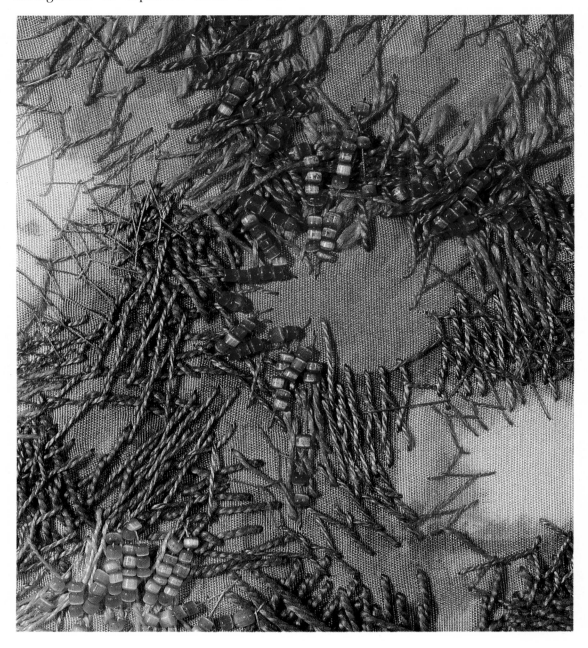

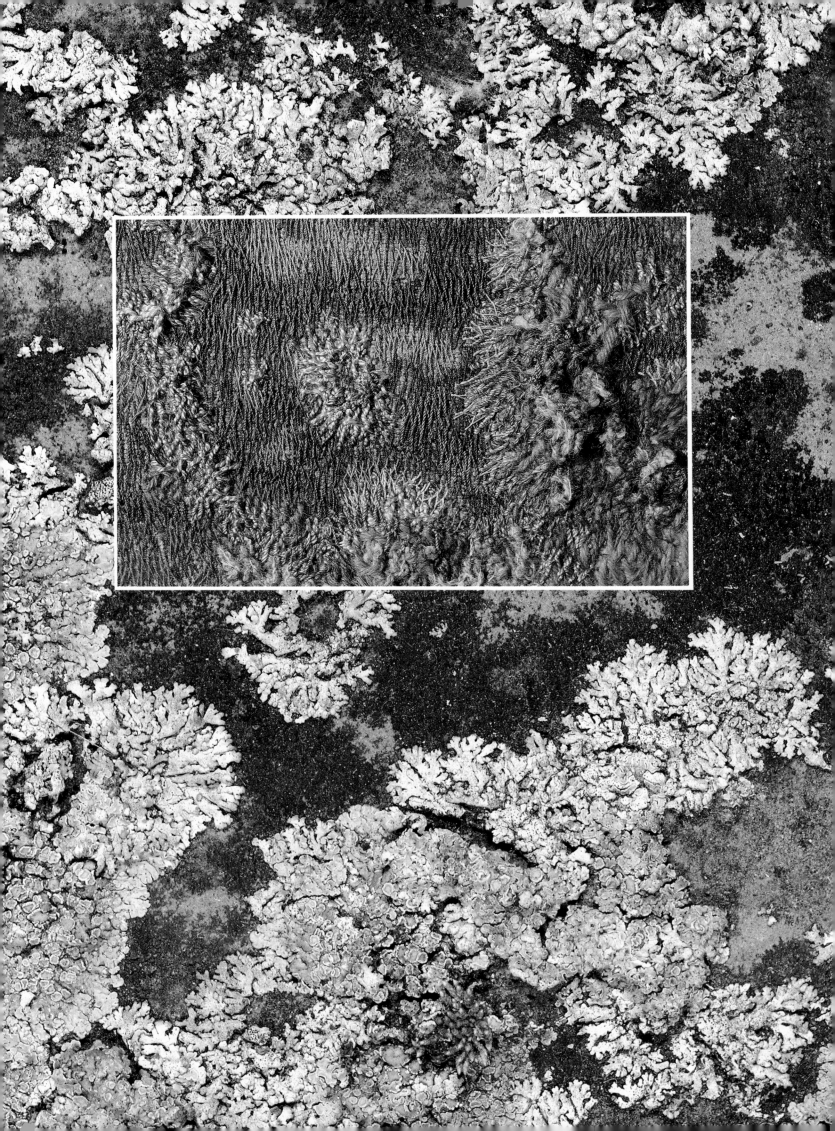

CROSS STITCH

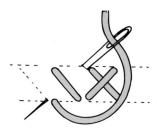

You will probably associate cross stitch with counted thread designs, which consist of evenly sized stitches in formal, often geometric, patterns. These can be extremely charming; however, a freer approach is great fun and can achieve beautifully coloured and subtle effects.

Initially, block in the main areas of your design with fairly bold cross stitches. When the overall shapes and colours have been indicated, add further stitching in finer threads, working on top of and in between the existing ones, blending in and creating richly coloured and textured surfaces. Remember that fine or woolly threads worked closely together tend to merge into the background, whereas shiny, twisted or stiff threads work up into more clearly defined stitches; these could be used to highlight particular areas of interest.

By forming the stitches in the same way throughout, so that all the lower threads slant in one direction and all the upper threads slant in the other, you will give the design a certain rhythm and unity, however varied the scale or haphazard the stitchery.

The design for 'Yellow and Purple Pansies' (right) was first blocked in with fabric paints, then built up with freely worked cross stitches in vibrantly coloured threads. The densely worked lines of cross stitch (above, right), using a variety of threads, yarns and fabric strips, were inspired by rock formations.

Opposite: *Patterns of brickwork, flintstone and moss (inset) have been interpreted in random cross stitches, using various threads and woven tapes on a grey fabric.*

FLY STITCH

Interpreting fly stitch in a variety of ways can be very exciting. You may have previously learned to work it only in the conventional manner, but it has many interesting variations. Do experiment with the spacing, length and arrangement of all parts of the stitch. Such experiments may well produce beautiful formal patterns or freer textural effects. For example, by elongating the central holding-down stitch, you can suggest tall grasses, as shown opposite. Solid geometric patterns can be achieved by blocking four or five stitches closely together, arranging them to form stripes, squares, diamonds or chevrons. By stitching several closely together, decreasing the size progressively, you could suggest leaf shapes. See what other configurations you can devise.

A field of rape flowers gone to seed (inset, opposite) has been interpreted in this fly stitch sampler, stitched in shiny and matt embroidery wools and cottons, with the holding-down stitches elongated. A totally different approach was used for the simplified floral/leaf motif (below), in which the stitches have been grouped in concentric and linear patterns. The transition from one motif to another has been smoothly accomplished by using matt, dark threads, which recede into the background.

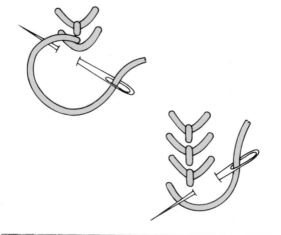

This brilliantly coloured geometric piece (below) shows another innovative use of fly stitch. Here the stitches – worked in silk and coton perlé *threads – are ingeniously stacked to form a rectangular pattern.*

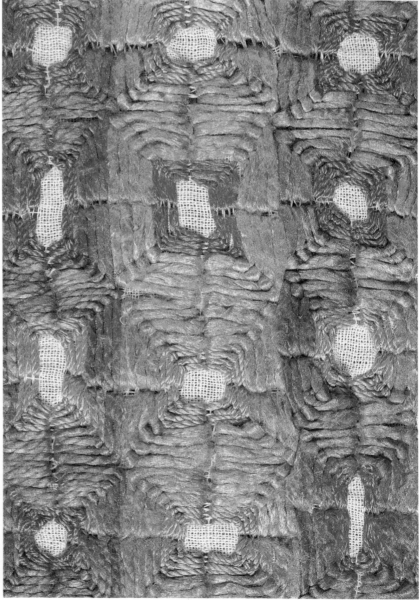

FRENCH KNOTS

Although working large areas of a design in this stitch can be time-consuming, everybody loves sewing French knots, and they certainly can give a pleasing textural quality to many pieces of embroidery. If you are working most or all of a design in French knots, one approach could be to block in part of your design first with knots worked in thick threads and then add finer, or perhaps shiny ones in and around the main areas.

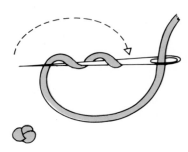

Conventionally, the thread is looped twice around the needle. For a rounder, neater result, use a thicker thread and one twist around the needle, keeping the loop quite taut as the needle is taken back through the cloth. Sometimes, however, knots worked incorrectly or in an irregular manner, with loops left protruding, can add further interest to the embroidery.

The appealing textures that can be created wih French knots are evident in these two examples (right and below). Gradations of scale can be achieved by varying the thickness of thread used, as in the yellow example; the stitch also lends itself to subtle colour harmonies, as in the example at right.

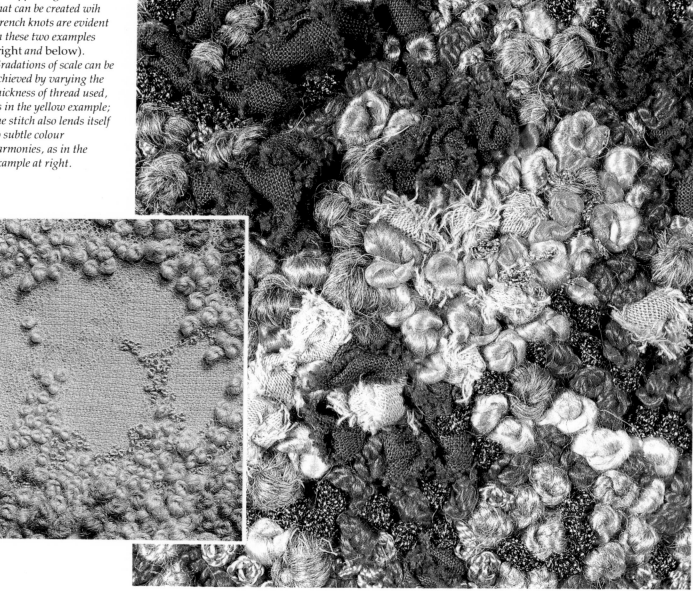